HIDDEN TREASURES

Unearthing the Goodness of God

Cindy Rickson

ISBN 979-8-89309-618-7 (Paperback)
ISBN 979-8-89309-619-4 (Digital)

Covenant Books
11661 Hwy 707
Murrells Inlet, SC 29576
www.covenantbooks.com

To my children and grandchildren
who keep me in reasons to stay on my
knees, pray, and seek the Lord.

CONTENTS

ACKNOWLEDGMENTS

Thank You, Father, that You know all about being a perfect parent.
Thank You, Lord Jesus, that You have walked
in the entirety of my human experience.
Thank You for Your Spirit that abides in me,
closer than when You walked the earth.
Thank You that nothing is hidden that will not be revealed.[1]
Thank You that You know my words before they are spoken.[2]
Thank You that You know the end from the beginning.[3]
Thank You for Your Spirit Who takes over when
I don't know what or how to pray.[4]
Thank You for
Kellie and William Stilianessis,
Heather and Justin Champagne,
Connor,
Liam,
Olivia,
Megan and Ben Rooks,
Lily,
Levi,
Jenna and Dreyton Caputo,

---

[1]   Luke 8:17
[2]   Psalm 139:4
[3]   Isaiah 46:10
[4]   Romans 8:26

Dominic,
Ryan,
Caitlin Elizabeth Rickson.

In loving memory of Ernest Mark Rickson, who showed us all the love of the Father.

INTRODUCTION

Being Led to Treasures

From silence and darkness to a cry of rescue and light. From complacency and comfort to a new way and foreign territory. This is a story of birth and growth and change. It is an account of hardships and renewed hope. How often we long to stay in a familiar place, but that's where stagnation happens. That's where bed sores develop. That's where pneumonia sets in. Just as an infant can't stay in the womb forever without harm, we must move from season to season. We are happy to see some seasons end. In others, we would like to camp out until Jesus returns. But Scripture clearly says there is a season for everything[1]—good and otherwise. And the Byrds backed that up in song![2]

Sometimes we get stuck, longing to go back. We would do well to heed the words of Jesus, "Remember Lot's wife"[3] recalling the account of Sodom.[4] Though this woman, named only as Lot's wife, was led by the hand of angels away from destruction to a place of safety, she looked back. Not only did she look back, she also looked back longingly, intently, with pleasure.[5] Even though what was behind her was nothing but an ash heap, she longed for it. The result

---

[1] Ecclesiastes 3:1
[2] "Turn! Turn! Turn!" by the Byrds
[3] Luke 17:32
[4] Genesis 19:26
[5] Strong's concordance #5027, NABAT

was that she became a pillar of salt, stuck between destruction and the promise.

The Israelites looked back when the going got rough at the Red Sea in Exodus 14. They accused Moses of bringing them into the wilderness to die. They were sure that their life was over, that this was the end of the road. Have you ever been there? Do you suppose that when the birth process starts, that is what a baby thinks? "Well, it's all over now. I am never going to survive this trip!" And the mother may have the same thoughts.

We know that the journey a baby takes at birth is to a much better place. It is a place to experience things that they never dreamed possible in the womb. The same was true of the Israelites. Moses was leading them to God's Promised Land. The journey would be hard, but something much better awaited them on the other side. That's the promise God makes to us with many hidden treasures along the way. But our natural tendency is to freak out. At least mine is!

God spoke to Moses when the people pushed back. He said, "Why do you cry to Me? Tell the children of Israel to go forward."[6] The original Hebrew word for "go forward" is *nasa*.[7] Now, I don't know if the space program researched that, but I do know that the word means to get off the launching pad, explore new places, move on because there is more.

That is our mission, but God is not going to drag us along against our will. He doesn't want robotic children. Psalm 23 says that the Good Shepherd "*leads* me beside still waters."[8] Sheep are very skittish animals. They are not very smart and are in desperate need of a shepherd for survival. In order for sheep to drink, they need to kneel down on their front legs. This puts them into a very vulnerable position against enemies. They must trust the shepherd for protection. The shepherd needs to find still water because the sheep won't kneel at raging waters. They fear being swept away in moving water especially if their coat is thick. The shepherd must provide a peaceful

---

[6] Exodus 14:15
[7] Strong's concordance #5265, NASA
[8] Psalm 23:2

and safe environment for them to drink, and the sheep must trust him.

The Shepherd also "*leads* me in the path of righteousness."[9] He doesn't drive them from behind with a whip. He says, "This is the way, walk in it."[10] The paths on which the shepherds of Israel lead their flock are not lush, wide, flat paths as often depicted. They are rocky, narrow paths up the mountainsides to the places where the shepherd has prepared a grazing place for them. The sheep need to stay on the narrow path close to the shepherd or risk stumbling off the side of the cliffs.

The journey of the sheep is scary yet rewarding. It requires the loving hand and guidance of the shepherd for the sheep to survive. It requires that the sheep follow him. Scripture says that we are His sheep.[11] The more we come to know the truth about our Shepherd, the easier it is to trust Him and follow Him as His sheep. He will not corral us. He has given us free will, and He wants us to come to Him willingly. He invites us to come especially when we're scared and lost.[12]

He doesn't want us to be afraid of Him. He wants us to be afraid of offending Him because of the love He has for us. Because He has given me free will, I can choose to go my own way. What I fear the most is that He will give me over to my carnal desires if I persist in resisting Him.[13] Thankfully, He knows my heart.[14]

So the journey may be long. There may be traps and snares along the way. I may need to step over some rocks, but He promises me green pastures, still waters, and right paths if I stick with Him. This is the story of a journey. I invite you to come along with me and you honor me by doing so.

This is a look back, not longingly with desire to go back. Who wants to end up a mossy, human salt lick with bed sores and pneu-

---

9 Psalm 23:3
10 Isaiah 30:21
11 Psalm 100:3
12 Matthew 11:28
13 Romans 1:28
14 1 Samuel 16:7

monia? No, this is a look back to gain wisdom so that I don't fall into the same traps again and again. Perhaps it will free you from the same.

It is a look back to see the altars built by stones of remembrance. God instructed Joshua to collect stones from the dried-up Jordan river to serve as a reminder that the hand of God is mighty.[15] I once did a Bible study by one of my favorite authors, Beth Moore. One of the assignments was to create a timeline of my life and mark dates where God was undeniably present even before I knew Him. I marked those events with gold paint so that they look like altars. The most life-changing revelation in that assignment was that I realized that even before I was born, God created the man who I would marry who would show me the love of God and demonstrate the love of a good father. Even before I was born, God had a good plan for me. My timeline is visible evidence of His presence. Looking back makes me even more grateful as I see His mighty hand. I see that He has been there all along, even when I couldn't see Him.

It is a look back to testify of the faithfulness of my Shepherd. I have asked Him to be my Shepherd, and He asks you to do the same. Unless we make Him our own, He cannot lead us. Your shepherd cannot lead me, and my Shepherd cannot lead you. We, as sheep, must know His voice and know that He knows us each by name.[16] We are not just one of the herd. We are His.

So thank you for joining me on this treasure hunt. Sometimes the treasures are right on the surface. Sometimes, it takes some serious digging. But He is faithful. That is my testimony!

Father, Your words are the truth that bring freedom.[17] I pray that the words of my testimony will glorify You. I pray that as You are lifted up, You will draw the reader to Yourself, to know You for Who You really are and who we are in You.

---

[15] Joshua 4:21–24
[16] John 10:27
[17] John 8:32

PART 1

Treasures in Small Packages

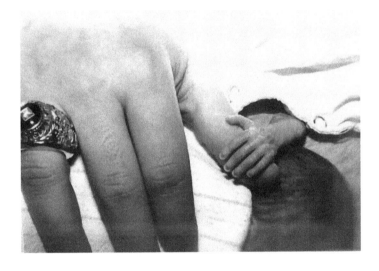

Photo Credit: Phyllis Scribner

For who has despised the day of small things?
—Zechariah 4:10

CHAPTER 1

My Life as a NICU Nurse

Some people need to search long and hard for what they want to be when they grow up. This was never a question for me. From a very young age, I wanted to be a nurse. I never had much exposure to the medical field, but I was certain that that was what I wanted to do. It was my inborn calling. I was not interested in an administrative position. I wanted my hands in the trenches, so to speak. A hospital-based diploma nursing program was perfect for me. It would allow me to start practicing while I learned, and I could be ready for "real life" in three years. The two programs closest to me were full until the next school year. Patience has always been a steep learning curve for me! I didn't want to wait so I chose a program in Springfield, Massachusetts. Little did I know how all this would transform into the perfect plan that God had for me, even before I really knew Him.

Babies were also my passion, so I naturally gravitated toward pediatrics. I spent the required year practicing medical nursing after graduation before a job opened up with growing premature babies and eventually in the neonatal intensive care unit (NICU). I had found my niche and ended up spending thirty years there.

Life in the NICU can be very quiet and sedate, but it can change very quickly with the emergent needs of another little life. The ultimate goal in the care of babies born ill or before their expected date of delivery is to replicate life in the womb as much as possible. An incubator or Isolette serves that purpose. The fluorescent lights in the nursery are kept dim, the noise level kept to a minimum, blankets cover warm incubators to shield out natural light, sometimes soft music or a recording of a parent's voice plays very softly inside. When the baby needs to be awakened for care, hands are placed gently on them so as not to startle them. Soft words are spoken to let them know you are there; and the task of vital signs, weighing, diapering, feeding and administering medication and treatments begins. Once resettled, the infant may be repositioned with blanket boundaries to keep their arms and legs close to their little bodies to maintain the feeling of prenatal security.

NICU babies are monitored continually both by machines and watchful eyes. When an infant forgets to breathe or their heart rate drops below a designated setting, an alarm will sound. A gentle back rub will typically remind them to breathe or stimulate their heart rate. Premature babies need to be left undisturbed and allowed to sleep a majority of the time in order for them to grow and develop, but they require constant attention to any interruption in their vital signs.

Babies do not breathe air in the womb. Their lungs are filled with amniotic fluid. Oxygen is supplied to the baby by way of the maternal placenta until birth. When a baby takes its first breath at birth, it is like blowing up a balloon for the first time. With the proper maturity and development, the subsequent breaths take less effort. Premature babies, however, have lungs that are not mature enough to function efficiently outside of the womb, independent of their mother. Each breath takes significant energy, and these babies typically require respiratory assistance. The administration of oxygen is very carefully monitored so it does not cause damage to their still-developing eyes and other organs.

The premature baby is stressed by being out in the world before the end of gestation. When properly cared for, however, their lungs can grow and mature; and they become better able to overcome respiratory challenges. Gradually, they are able to build up a little fat on their body to better control their temperature. Their nervous system matures so they are reminded to breathe and keep a stable heart rate and blood pressure. Their blood vessels become less fragile, so they are less likely to experience bleeding in their brain caused by the stress of life outside the womb. Their gut becomes mature enough to tolerate milk instead of being dependent on intravenous feeding. It is all a very delicate process that cannot be rushed. It requires patience, skill, and great attention to detail.

Another aspect of NICU nursing is travelling by ambulance to outlying community hospitals for sick infants to bring them back for intensive care. This involves preparing in advance to assure all the necessary equipment is packed to provide care for the infant in a place that is not equipped for such care. Any missing equipment can have harmful, if not catastrophic, effects on a fragile, new life. The priority is to stabilize the baby before beginning the trip back to the NICU. Telemedicine has made great advances in this kind of care. Oftentimes, some kind of stabilization can begin even before the transport team's arrival. Before telemedicine, however, it was often a surprise to see what awaited our arrival.

The job of the NICU nurse back in the nursery is to support these fragile infants through the critical periods of growth by assessing when they might be headed for a medical crisis. Subtle changes in color, vital signs, lab results, behavior, feeding tolerance, or tolerance for being handled are just a few ways the infant may signal trouble. Responding to changes skillfully can help to avoid a major medical crisis that can affect the infant and their family for many years to come.

Parents are also in need of the care of the NICU nurse. The environment can be crowded with machines, unfamiliar noises, and a very strange and foreign vocabulary. Acceptance and orientation into this new and unexpected "home" for their new baby is crucial. The cacophony of sights and sounds in this unwanted home must be redirected so that parents can see a real baby, *their* baby, in the midst of the equipment, medical jargon, prognoses, and staff. Parents can be empowered to be a part of the care team by learning the benefit of hands-off, silence care, or helping with care when their baby is able. A mom can provide precious milk to nourish her baby when the time is right, giving her a unique purpose when she may feel like a "helpless" parent. When the time is right for kangaroo care, the baby snuggles in, skin to skin, to the warmth and love of a parent who may have waited patiently for many unpredictable days or weeks for this intimate contact. Through the gains and setbacks, hopes and fears, celebrations and crises, a crucial goal of the NICU nurse is to support a family, promoting confidence and nurturing delicate bonding in their unique situation. Some families are fortunate enough to take home a happy and healthy baby. Some learn to love and care for babies with great challenges. Some experience the short lifetime of their baby without leaving the NICU. They may leave the hospital with empty arms and broken dreams. I have seen, however, that even the shortest lives are not without a purpose and a lasting imprint on a family. Whatever the outcome, it is always a privilege and great responsibility to be a part of their "family," a time that most families never forget.

For thirty years, I tried not to take that privilege for granted or take that responsibility lightly. There came a time when I could no longer give it my all, so I moved on but not without great appreciation for all I learned both professionally and spiritually. You see, when we invite Jesus to be Lord, He breathes His life-giving breath into us, empowering and enabling us to experience the life that He gives and the life that pleases Him.[1] The more we invite the breath of His Spirit in and depend on Him, the easier the effort becomes to follow Him. The incubator of God's presence keeps us within safe boundaries, free from the chilling, deafening, and blinding world around us. To be safe, we must choose to stay "in" Him. He keeps a continual, watchful, and protective eye on us; and He knows the subtle changes that signal that we are headed for crisis. When we forget to breathe, falling into a state of lethargy, He sounds the alarm, reminding us to wake up. When our hearts slow from fatigue, He will gently stimulate us back to activity. Some seasons may feel like hands-off isolation, but they can lead to closeness and warmth as we continue to grow in Him, nourished by the milk of His Word.[2] If we find ourselves in an outlying place that is ill equipped for our needs, He comes to rescue us. He is careful to stabilize us where we are

---

[1]   Philippians 2:13
[2]   1 Peter 2:2

before moving us closer to the care we need. He doesn't rush in and bullishly try to change our lives. Rather, He gently knocks, letting us know He is there to provide what we need and to do what only He can do. His "treatments" are always carefully and individually administered to be therapeutic, not harmful.[3] He allows us periods of rest after trials so that we can regain our strength, swaddled in His security. His voice can always be heard in the quiet if we choose to listen and He patiently waits for us to be "ready" for the closeness of His embrace to hear His heartbeat.

Becoming part of the family of God can be a strange and stretching experience as well, learning a new language and new ways. It may seem foreign at first but the care and skill of those who have walked this way before us helps us to grow and mature and better understand this new way. Little by little, we build up our tolerance and are better able to control ourselves in what we perceive as stressful situations. Some of us walk this journey with few hindrances. Others learn to walk with a limp all the way home. We never outgrow our need for Him, and we are never out of the attention of the One Who created us, sustains us, rescues us from crisis, holds us close to Himself, nourishes us, and loves us unconditionally. He is committed to and able to do His job for eternity without fail. He is always faithful to bring us treasures from what we see as small packages. In the following pages, you will read about some of those treasures.

Father, thank You for the intricacies of Your creation. Thank You for Your constant care and concern of every detail of our lives. We are not hidden from You, and You know exactly what we need exactly when we need it. Help us to trust You more and more and to be hidden in You[4] for Your glory.

"For you created my inmost being; you knit me together in my mother's womb. I praise you because I am fearfully and wonderfully made; your works are wonderful; I know that full well" (Psalm 139:13–14).

---

[3] Jeremiah 29:11
[4] Colossians 3:3

CHAPTER 2

The Cry

As NICU nurses, we were expected to be present at potentially high-risk deliveries to assist in resuscitation, if needed. As a result, I have had the privilege of witnessing many, many births. No matter how many times I have seen it, I have always been in awe of the transformation of life at birth. To see a purple, cyanotic, lifeless form come to life is nothing short of miraculous. To hear that cry and see color turn to pink always left me breathless with expectation and relieved, all at the same time. To understand the physiology of that transition makes it all the more miraculous.

The circulatory system and the respiratory system of babies before and after birth are completely different. Before birth, babies do not breathe air. Oxygen is supplied to the developing infant by way of the placenta and umbilical cord. The mother is the one who supplies the lifeline. While in the womb, babies' lungs are filled with amniotic fluid. It is gradually absorbed as the expected date of delivery approaches, preparing them for the birth transition. The process of birth compresses the lungs to expel whatever fluid may be remaining. A surgical birth does not have that benefit which may cause distress at birth. A premature birth is further complicated by immature lungs, unable to bear the burden of life outside the womb.

At birth, the baby is moved from a dark, warm, protected environment to a world that is colder, brighter and full of stimulation. This causes the baby to gasp, taking their first breath. When this happens, it signals the circulatory system to change from prenatal life, fully dependent on the blood supply of the mother, to life apart from her. The lungs fill with air and the baby transitions to their own circulatory system to deliver oxygen. This is what causes the baby to change from a purple, lifeless form to pink, screaming and flailing. The placenta has now reached the end of its purpose and must be separated to protect both the baby and the mom from excessive blood loss. To understand the complexity of these vital changes is to understand, in part, the complexity of God and His creative ability. It is truly miraculous and is so often taken for granted.

When those changes do not take place in the perfect time and in the perfect sequence, it becomes a critical event. When that cry is not heard, it commonly causes a deafening and dreadful silence and sets the rescue into motion.

In Scripture, between Malachi, the last book in the First Testament and Matthew, the first book in the New Testament, there was a deafening and dreadful silence.

There had been no word from God for four hundred years. The prophets were silent. God's people waited in slavery and oppression by the Roman government for their rescue. They waited, expecting to hear the snort of a war horse or the sound of a battle cry to signal their deliverance. Instead, they heard the life cry of an Infant. This was the sound of God's plan of rescue. The people wanted a warrior to overthrow Rome. God sent a Baby to overthrow sin. The deadly silence of separation from God because of sin was broken by the rescue cry of a Baby to bring us life and renewed fellowship with God.

This Baby was not born in the cleanliness and control of a delivery room. No, this Baby was born into poverty to a young, inexperienced, unwed couple in the filth and squalor of an animal shelter. He was not placed in a warm, soft bed but rather He slept in an animal feeding trough lined with prickly hay. This was not what anyone expected.

I wonder what it was like for Jesus to wait? He waited four thousand years after the fall of man. He waited through four hundred years of God's silence, seeing and hearing the ignorance and disobedience of His children, seeing the oppression and bondage of sin unremedied by the law, seeing the utter darkness of the world He had created. Jesus waited until the Father said, "Now!"[1]

I wonder what it was like for Jesus to choose to leave the glories of heaven and step into the gutter of our world, to choose to leave the perfection and adoration of heaven knowing that He would be doubted, despised, and put to death to redeem the very people who caused Him so much agony. What was it like for the Light of the world to be surrounded by darkness. What kind of love allowed Him to choose to live with us so He wouldn't have to live without us? What kind of joy would allow Him to endure the cross,[2] hell, and the grave? What kind of humility would cause Him to leave the limitless bounds of time and space and choose to be confined in a virgin womb for nine months, growing under the beat of the heart He had created and set into motion? What kind of obedience would cause Him to choose to be subjected to the limits of a human body, experiencing everything we feel so that He could empathize[3] with us and intercede for us[4] at the throne of grace? He knows every experience we have had or will have from hunger and thirst to joy and sorrow to temptation and strength to acceptance and rejection, inclusive of the entire human experience. What kind of trust enabled Him to wait until the fullness of time[5] to come to our rescue? What kind of restraint would allow Him to keep His true identity under wraps until His hour had come?[6] What kind of forgiveness and compassion would allow Him to not call down fire from heaven[7] in response to rejection and ridicule? What kind of confidence would restrain Him

---

[1] Galatians 4:4
[2] Hebrews 12:2
[3] Hebrews 4:15
[4] Hebrews 7:25
[5] Galatians 4:4
[6] John 2:4
[7] Luke 9:54

from calling on legions of angels[8] to rescue Him from crucifixion? What kind of patience would allow Him to continue to knock on the door of our hearts when we continually ignore our need for Him?

When Jesus came, many of the ancients stuck to their own expectations and missed the miracle of that cry that signaled our rescue. They chose to continue to search for the Messiah that they had created in their own image instead of the one the Father sent as His exact representation.[9] Even when Jesus had proved His divinity by signs and miracles, they continued to overlook Him and search for the God of their own expectation. The cry of Jesus is intended to transition us from the death of the separation from God to a life unlike the one from which we came. Do you hear His cry? Are we willing to set aside our own expectations and allow Him to reveal Who He really is and allow the transition that will bring life?

What was it like for the fully divine to become fully human?[10] Jesus waited. Jesus came, and He is coming back for us. I am grateful for the cry of His rescue that transitioned me from a world without God to His world of peace. I can depend on His lifeline and not my own. It is kind of a reverse birth process, a rebirth. My own strength wears out very quickly, but His strength never fails. And He desires that I cling to and rely on Him for everything. After all, He is the source of every heartbeat and every breath that He has allowed me to have. Let it be used for His glory.

Father, thank You for the gift of life—for my life and the lives of my loved ones. Thank You for those lives that are now with You, waiting for our reunion because of Your saving grace. It is truly miraculous and not to be ignored or taken for granted.

> For You formed my inward parts;
> You covered me in my mother's womb.

---

[8]   Matthew 26:53
[9]   Hebrews 1:3
[10] Colossians 2:9

I will praise You, for I am fearfully and
wonderfully made;
Marvelous are Your works, And that my
soul knows very well.
(Psalm 139:13–14)

"I came so that they would have life, and
have it abundantly."
(John 10:10)

CHAPTER 3

His Voice

My relational walk with the Lord began as a young wife, mother, and intensive care nursery nurse in Massachusetts. I had grown up in a denominational church; and as a young adult, my prayers had become empty words, and my actions were heartless rituals. I knew there was more than just vain repetitions,[1] but I didn't know where to find it. The Bible says, "The Lord utters His Voice,"[2] but I had yet to "hear" it.

Before I entered into a personal relationship with the Lord, I did, however, "hear His Voice" one day. I was a freshman nursing student, on my own for the first time. I had strict expectations imposed by the school, so my boundaries were clearly mapped. I was out walking alone on the streets of Springfield one Sunday morning. I had walked past a Hispanic Catholic church when I "heard" the Lord's prompting, "Go in." I did not speak Spanish, and I did not speak Catholic. I had grown up in the Episcopal Church, so I was not totally unfamiliar with the program. I went in and sat in silence during the mass. I can't say that anything spectacular happened that day, other than I returned to the dorm safely; and I was, in the future, protected from many subsequent risks that I took out of ignorance. I do, however, recall this as the beginning of His calling me to Himself.

---

[1] Matthew 6:7
[2] Jeremiah 25:30; Joel 2:11, 3:16; Amos 1:2

The first time I was sure I heard the Lord's voice occurred as I was reading a book my mother had given me. It was titled *How to Live Like a King's Kid*[3] by Harold Hill. It was very simply written and easy to apply. At the end of the book, there was a challenge to pray something like this:

> Lord, I don't know what I'm doing here, but I'm going to do it anyway. I need something more, and You said to ask. I am asking You to take over my life and be my Lord. I know I don't deserve it based on anything I have done. But I do know that You died on the cross and rose from the dead so that I could be forgiven and made right with God. So I am asking to be a part of Your family because of what You have done for me. Make me a King's kid.

Nothing really changed at first. There were no fireworks or angelic sightings. There was, however, a growing hunger to read the Bible and learn about the One I had asked to be my Lord. I wanted to know what pleased Him and what He wanted of me and for me. God has been faithful to continually show me all this in His Word from that day forward. My husband, Ernie was not as searching as I was, so reading the Bible was something I did in secret. I didn't want him to think I was some kind of freak. I was slowly becoming someone different than the one he had married, and I didn't want to scare him off. I guess, at that point, I was more afraid of displeasing him than displeasing the Lord. So when Ernie was out with his friends, I would put the kids to bed and dig out my Bible. Even in my hiding, however, the Lord was drawing me out.

Shortly thereafter, I was winding up my three-to-eleven evening shift in the nursery. I was preparing to make the transition from nurse back to wife and mommy, hoping to catch some sleep before

---

[3] Harold Hill, *How To Live Like A King's Kid* (Bridge-Logos, 1974).

that transition made any great demands on me. I was minding my own business, not feeling at all "spiritual."

The nursing supervisor approached me and, merely in a manner of conversation, related to me an incident that she had just encountered. The parents of one of our babies had phoned the priest to request that he come and pray for their baby son, Rory. I did not know Rory or his parents, but it was evident that he was not doing well, judging by the number of staff that had been at his bedside most of the evening. The priest had denied the family a visit, justifying that he had already baptized the baby a few days ago. He did agree to stop in to see Rory and his parents the next morning on his appointed (but certainly, in my opinion, not anointed) rounds. The parents were not pleased with this arrangement and, in their desperation, had contacted the nursing supervisor.

The longer I mulled this situation over in my mind, the more disturbed I became. I kept thinking that we had taken this baby away from his parents and put him in this incredibly terrifying environment, justifiably for his own well-being. We had "allowed" his parents to see him, but their interaction or even their time with him was severely limited due to his fragile medical condition. Thankfully, conditions and expectations in the intensive care nursery have changed drastically in the last four decades. At that time, however, parents had little involvement and were granted limited access to their infants. Rory's parents could not *do* anything tangible for their son to secure his future and the medical options were failing. The only viable option remaining for them was to pray.

I questioned in my mind how the priest could assume that Rory would still be among the living in the morning. As a nurse, I had repeatedly been questioned about the true urgency of an emergency baptism. Could it wait until morning? How do you answer that question? Only God knows the number of our days.[4] I concluded that if this was the way we were going to offer pastoral care, perhaps we should do everyone a favor and not offer it at all. I can't say for sure

---

[4] Psalm 37:18

if this was self-righteousness or righteous indignation, but it caused me to move.

Even though I can't say that I "heard" the Lord's voice, I found myself, without much more thought, in Rory's mother's hospital room. I explained to both parents that they didn't know me, and this probably sounded crazy to them but their problem had been brought to my attention. I suggested that maybe there was a way that I could help. Within a half an hour, in the wee hours of the night, the minister from the church I attended joined Rory's parents and me around his incubator and prayed together on his behalf. Finally, Rory's parents had been able to *do* something for their very ill, tiny, helpless son. It was a small act of obedience on all our parts, but it had a profound effect on each one of us.

Rory did live until the next morning. In fact, he went home a few months later. He still had significant handicaps to overcome, but the bond that that act of faith in God created between his family and me existed for many years. I thank God that He cared enough for all of us to "carry" me to that hospital room, to show the incredible power of His love. Though the audible voice of the Lord was not a reality for me, He picked me up bodily to do His good and perfect will. It was as if He knew my heart was right, but my mind and body were not fully ready to follow through. God led me by His Spirit in spite of myself and I was forever changed. This truth was demonstrated: "For it is God who works in you both to will and to do for His good pleasure."[5]

That simple yet profound act of being carried by the Lord steadily grew into my stumbling with Him to walking and running with Him and often back to stumbling or even being carried again. But the Lord, in His unfailing mercy, has always picked me up and dusted me off. He continues on with me and allows me to continue on with Him. His voice has become more and more discernable to me as the years have passed. It becomes more and more clear as I have continued to learn to tune out the distracting noises in my head and around me and tune into Him. A physical manifestation of my act

---

5   Philippians 2:13

of faith on Rory's behalf was noted by my colleagues. It was noted mostly in jest, but it was, nonetheless, noted. About the same time, a popular commercial for dog food was seen on television. It claimed that if your dog ate a certain brand of dog food, he would exhibit the "high-pro glow." This was depicted by a dog romping through an open field surrounded by a circle of glowing light that followed him everywhere and even appeared to make him smile. That's how my colleagues described my appearance from that time on. "Watch out. Cindy's getting that high-pro glow again." Though I had, I confess, feared being labelled a Jesus freak, my colleagues did not ridicule my childlike act of faith. God's purpose for us is to shine as lights in the world.[6] At that time, I had only a glimpse of His power at work within me, and I had not yet "heard" a word.

Jesus had a similar high-pro glow experience recorded by Matthew in chapter 17 and confirmed by Peter, an eyewitness.[7] In this account, Jesus was transfigured.[8] In the Greek, the word for transfigured[9] is similar to our word for metamorphosis. It involves a change in nature by supernatural means. It means changing form in keeping with inner reality. We know that Jesus was God incarnate, God in human flesh.[10] At that moment, Jesus was temporarily changed in His physical nature of flesh. His clothes became as white as the light and His face shone like the sun. His complete divine nature overcame His earthly nature so that what was inside was completely visible on the outside. His divinity overcame His humanity. The voice of God spoke identifying Jesus as His beloved Son.

God desires for us, His children, to be transformed more and more into His image. Because we were created in His image,[11] it is our inner reality. This image was obscured by sin at the fall of man in Genesis chapter 3, but Jesus came to restore our God-given image

---

[6] Philippians 2:15
[7] 2 Peter 1:18
[8] Matthew 17:2
[9] Strong's concordance #3339, METAMORPHOO
[10] Colossians 2:9
[11] Genesis 1:27

by conforming us to His image.[12] The sin with which we are now born because of that fall causes us to be self-centered as opposed to God-centered.

If you have ever taken care of an infant, you have witnessed self-centeredness. No one else exists outside of the immediate needs of that baby. God's intent is that we outgrow our self-focus to see and interact with the world around us in a positive and life-giving way. That is what Jesus did. He showed us a way out of ourselves. His way transforms us from self-centeredness to God and other-centeredness. We are not the master of our own destiny. We are not our own boss. We do not live for our own comfort and pleasure alone. He gave His life so we could have life abundantly[13] in Him and share it with others. The longer and more intentionally we walk with Jesus, following His example and His Words, the more the smudges of sin are erased. We are continually transfigured to let His light shine through in the darkness.

Thank You for Your light shining through me, Father. It is my heart's desire that those You bring in my path will see less and less of me and more and more of the light of Your Holy Spirit within me. Help me to become transparent so that Your love, Your power, and Your mercy can flow unhindered to others through this earthen vessel. I seek a mind through which You can think, a heart through which You can love, a voice through which You can speak, hands through which You can work and feet to bring Your peace, a vessel through which You can be glorified in the Name of Jesus.

"Let your light shine before others, that they may see your good deeds and glorify your Father in heaven" (Matthew 5:16).

---

[12] Romans 8:29
[13] John 10:10

CHAPTER 4

Unbelief

God's Word says, "If you have faith as small as a mustard seed, you can say to this mountain, 'Move from here to there' and it will move. Nothing will be impossible for you."[1]

Even as a baby Christian, with wobbly legs and faith barely the size of a mustard seed, the Lord demonstrated this truth for me. As I was learning to be a "King's kid,"[2] I was intrigued by Mr. Hill's real life, honest approach to living in the faith according to the Word of God. It instantly sparked my interest and curiosity. He not only offered an invitation to be a King's kid but also to step out of our "educated think tank." His story related to healing. This intrigued me since my part time life was with families in crisis in the intensive care nursery. It was here, in this mission field, that the Lord provided an opportunity to put this challenge into practice.

My assignment for the evening was to care for a full-term baby girl who had an idiopathic cyst on her lung. That simply means that they didn't know it's origin or what the long-term effects would be. What was certain was that it impaired her breathing. She would likely need complicated and risky surgery to correct the problem. My heart became almost unbearably burdened for this baby and her family. There was no logical reason to explain this burden as the nurs-

---

[1] Matthew 17:20
[2] Harold Hill, *How To Live Like A King's Kid* (Bridge-Logos, 1974).

ery was always full of hurting families. Something was special about this family and God "told" me to pray. Harold Hill had instructed me, using the Scriptures, how to pray in this situation. There was no magical prayer process or protocol. I just prayed from my heart, setting aside the vain repetitions that I had learned in my childhood.

Laying my hands on her, I prayed: "Lord, I'm not sure exactly what I'm doing here. You know it's just me standing here asking for Your favor for this baby. Perhaps an anointed pastor or even my mother would be better able to say what needs to be said here. Having no eloquent words or fancy prayers, I only stand on Your Word. Your Word says that if I ask You to heal this baby, You will. Thank You that Your heart breaks for her and her family even more than mine does. You trained me up as a nurse and this kind of 'treatment' is foreign to me. Imagine what a stir it would cause if I documented on her medical record that my plan of care included prayer and the laying on of hands. This is not how I was educated, but I am choosing You over my educated think tank. Everyone else seems to be at a loss as to what kind of medical intervention she needs. You are the Great Physician, so I place her in Your loving hands. Please, in Your infinite mercy, heal her now. Even though my mind tells me that this is crazy, I'm standing on Your Word, in Jesus's name. Amen."

The next evening, I cared for this baby again. Her chest X-ray had been repeated that morning, and her cyst was gone! She was breathing easier, and eventually, she went home without any problems. What an incredible testimony to the power and mercy of an Almighty God Who depends solely on the desperate need of His children! Unfortunately, I never saw her family again to share that testimony. But perhaps this was a testimony for me. The Lord convinced me that day, beyond a shadow of a doubt, that He does heal today just as He did when He walked this earth. Even when I was dripping with doubt and uncertainty, God reached down by way of His powerful Holy Spirit and made that baby whole. He confirmed His Word. "If we are faithless, He remains faithful."[3] In addition to

---

[3] 2 Timothy 2:13

healing this baby physically, God was working on healing my doubt and unbelief.

Needless to say, the medical staff was at a loss to explain this miraculous recovery, but they tried anyway. My past attempts to credit God for His work were feeble and fumbling and fell on deaf ears. We are sometimes so darkened in our own understanding,[4] knowledge and ability that the concept of giving credit elsewhere is unthinkable and certainly not scientific. Nonetheless, I was being obedient to a heavy burden that God had placed on my heart. Through this, He showed me not only His power but also His love and compassion for the hurting.

Jesus illustrates this in the Gospel of Mark.[5] A man brings his son to Jesus's disciples for healing of a seizure condition. The disciples are unable to cast out the spirit responsible for the boy's condition. But Jesus told the father, "Everything is possible for him who believes."[6] The boy's father responded, "I do believe; help me overcome my unbelief!"[7] Jesus cast out the spirit that caused the boy to be tormented but the boy then appeared dead. I wonder how long that lasted. It certainly was long enough for "many" people to declare him dead.[8] But Jesus took the boy by the hand, helped him up, and the boy stood up healed. It seems that there was enough time for unbelief to be revealed and then for belief to take hold.

Is it possible that the father's confession of unbelief was key to accessing the power of God? When the disciples questioned Jesus as to their inability to heal this boy, Jesus made it clear that it requires "prayer and fasting."[9] Some texts omit the fasting part. Whatever the case, the point is that both prayer and fasting change our focus from ourselves to God. We cannot heal anyone in our own power. We must acknowledge and rely on the healing power of the Healer. When we come humbly to Him and acknowledge that it is not our

---

4   Ephesians 4:18
5   Mark 9:14–29
6   Mark 9:23
7   Mark 9:24
8   Mark 9:26
9   Mark 9:29

fumbling words or our wavering faith that heals but He alone that heals, He acts to glorify Himself, to confirm that He is God, and we are not.

That is such good news for many of us. We know we don't know how to pray eloquently. Max Lucado says it this way: "Our prayers may be awkward. Our attempts may be feeble. But since the power of prayer is in the One who hears it and not in the one who speaks it, our prayers do make a difference."

I have prayed for many more healings since that day. Some prayers were answered as I expected. Others were answered outside my expectations. But they were all answered by the sovereignty of a loving God who desires our trust and dependence on Him. For me, this is still a work in progress. It has been a life-long process as He continues to replace my doubt and unbelief and my puny faith with awe and gratitude.

I stumbled at one point on the belief that I could manipulated the hand of God with my words. This was during the time of my husband, Ernie's battle with melanoma. My brothers and sisters in Christ and I believed that if we only spoke in the faith of His healing, Ernie would be healed. If we did not consider the possibility of his death, he would be healed on earth. To speak otherwise, to consider the facts, was unbelief. While we were praying and Ernie's physical condition didn't appear to respond, a good friend and prayer partner advised that we needed to pray harder. I was not sure how to do that, but I was willing to try anything. We persevered in our "belief."

Ernie and I never spoke of the possibility of his death until only days before he died. One morning, after he had received a devastating result from his latest PET scan, he told me to go out and get a cemetery plot. Acting is sheer obedience, not even considering the reality of what I was doing, I did just that. We had so much more to say to each other, but time had run out as we had tried to force the hand of God to do what we desired.

Ernie's healing is in heaven, for which I am grateful. What I now know is that, as I pray, I must give room for God to do as *He* wills and not as I will. I may not understand, but I am asked to trust a God Who has proven Himself faithful to me time and time again.

Prayer is not an attempt to change God's mind. It is a deliberate act to align my mind and my will with the reality of Who He is, trusting His goodness even when I don't understand. In the original language, prayer means to exchange my desires and wishes for His.[10] It is considering all the possibilities and trusting the outcome to Him.

Jesus Himself taught us how to pray:

> Your kingdom come.
> Your will be done
> On earth as it is in heaven.[11]

I believe Ernie and I would have been much better prepared for him to go if we had honestly faced all the possibilities. Scripture says that Abraham, "without weakening in his faith, he faced the fact that his body was as good as dead."[12] All the possibilities did not cause Abraham to lose his faith. He knew it was all about the power of God and not the power of his words before an omnipotent God. If Ernie and I had faced all the facts, not denying all the possibilities, we could have better supported each other in this journey together. Abraham's example of focusing on the God he trusted and not on what he desired, shows us how to strengthen our faith in the God of the impossible, no matter the outcome.

Jesus Himself demonstrated this in the garden of Gethsemane on His way to the cross. He prayed, "Father, if it is Your will, take this cup away from Me; NEVERTHELESS, not My will but Yours be done."[13] Jesus didn't deny that what was ahead would be agonizing. He did not "pray in faith" that it would not happen. No, He faced the facts, made His request known, and submitted to the perfect will of His Father. Jesus knew, intimately, that He could trust His Father. Jesus aligned His will with the Father's will. As a result, He was strengthened by an angel.[14] God didn't remove His trial, but He

---

[10] Strong's concordance #4336, PROSEUCHOMAI
[11] Matthew 6:10
[12] Romans 4:19 NIV
[13] Luke 22:42 (emphasis added)
[14] Luke 22:43

provided the strength and resolve necessary for Him to complete it. Jesus left us an example of the way to overcome the temptation to seek ease and comfort. If we pray the "nevertheless," He is faithful to equip and empower us for the "cup" ahead.

The more I come to know God, the clearer I hear His voice, the easier I allow Him to move my feet and my heart, and the more He proves to me that He is trustworthy.

Lord, I confess my unbelief. Thank You for making it undeniably clear to me how amazing You are to those who love You. Being unworthy in my own right to partake of Your miraculous works, I am so very grateful that, through Your Son, we can enter into Your kingdom right here on earth. Thank You that You care so much for every little detail of our lives. You not only cared for that little baby and her parents, but You also cared for me, hardened with doubt and uncertainty.

You knew what was ahead for me. Thank You for continuing to soften my heart so that I can trust you more and more. Thank You for showing me that it is words from the heart that You desire without planning or editing. These are acceptable in Your sight. Help me to remember, when the next obstacle comes, how powerful and loving You really are and how fully dependent I am on You.

> Let the words of my mouth and the meditation of my heart be acceptable in Your sight, O Lord, my strength and my Redeemer. (Psalm 19:14)

> But we have this treasure in earthen vessels, that the excellence of the power may be of God and not of us. (2 Corinthians 4:7)

CHAPTER 5

Growth

The Rickson family moved from Springfield, Massachusetts, to Vermont when I was still young in my personal walk with the Lord. This change was a powerful move of God, as it resulted in the salvation of my husband, Ernie and three daughters, Kellie, Heather, and Megan, as well as the addition of two more daughters, Jenna and Caitlin. Our Vermont home was new to my family, but it was the house in which I had grown up.

I use the phrase "grown up" in the physical sense alone as it becomes increasingly clear to me that growing up is a life-long process, especially as we grow in the Lord. When pondering what I want to be when I really grow up, it continually points in the direction of "attaining to the whole measure of the fullness of Christ."[1] I am continually learning that I won't be "grown up" until I meet Jesus face-to-face. It is my heart's desire that my heart will be worthy for His eyes to see. I am confident that it will be because of the work that He has done on my behalf. All I have needed to do is accept what He has already done. He is faithful to lead me through the growing process, each and every step of the way, making me the person He desires and created me to be.

As part of our new journey in Vermont, we were led by the faithful hand of God to a nondenominational Christian fellowship

---

[1] Ephesians 4:13

group. We had chosen to attend the Episcopal Church in which we were married when we first moved to Vermont, but God had a much greater plan for us. We originally attended this fellowship group as guests, but it eventually led us to a church family. The Christians in this church had an unashamed, burning love and desire to serve Jesus Christ. Their excitement was manifest in ways of worship and praise that were foreign to me, having been raised in and was still searching in the Episcopal Church.

Actually, most of my formative years had been spent standing backwards in the Episcopal Church. My mother would take my brother and me to church faithfully every Sunday. She would always seat us in one of the front pews. I was dressed in the traditional black patent leather shoes, white gloves, and a hat whether it was Easter or not. Invariably, no matter how hard I tried to be spic and span for church, I always missed a spot on my face. Perhaps it was the kind of spot that only a mother could discern, but week after week, it needed to be dealt with. The treatment for this spot was for my mother to spit on her gloved thumb and rub my face until the first layer of skin disappeared. Then, and only then, would I be presentable for church. This must have been one of those customs that automatically accompanies motherhood because I found myself doing the same to my own children, minus the gloves. They hated it as much as I did, but it was an involuntary response for me as a mom.

But let's go back to the point of standing backwards in church. My mother would seat us in one of the front pews, so the only way to see what was *really* going on in church was to stand backwards. I never saw those people in my childhood church showing their excitement for the Lord in quite the same way as our new church family did. And I had one of the best vantage points in the Episcopal Church for many years! No, all this was very new to me.

Our fellowship welcomed us into their fold with an overwhelming love and acceptance. Their genuine care and concern for us as we were going through trials with my teenage stepson was beyond refreshing. It was much closer to being vital to our survival. If they wanted to dance and raise their hands in praise to God, so be it. We had never had friends like this before. It was apparent that if we ever needed anything that was within their power to provide for us, we only needed to ask. In the same way, we were, over time, able to help them in their trials. In short, we praised God, studied His Word, cried, laughed, prayed with and for each other, ate together, stacked each other's wood and grew together as one body in a relatively short period of time. I learned what the body of Christ looked like in the flesh of everyday life. *This* was the thing for which I had been searching.

Jesus told us exactly how the world would know that we follow Him. He said that they will know we are His disciples if we love one another.[2] We entered this fellowship skeptical and tied to our old ways, but we soon experienced the love of God through our new friends. It's not that we didn't have friends before, but we were joined together with these friends as Christ followers. He was the motivation for what we did and that made all the difference. Our bond was in Him.

Their excitement was contagious. We soon became an indistinguishable part of that body of believers. We raised our family in this freedom of worship, and I still find it difficult to stand still when visiting more traditional churches. Being in fellowship with people so committed to Christ caused rapid and enormous growth for our entire family. Sometimes I still wonder how my reaching out in love to someone else can draw them closer to Christ. Then, I remember how these people drew us to Him. As I am obedient to be the hands and feet of Jesus, to speak His truth and pray for His guidance and leadership, He does all the work. He does the drawing.[3]

Ernie now worships directly at the throne of his Savior and we, his family, continue on as we learn to worship God in Spirit and in truth[4] here on earth. Our learning continues every day. We each have our own relationship with Jesus, and it all began with the seeds planted so strategically by a God who wants only the best for each of us. He can be trusted to complete the work He has begun.[5]

---

2 John 13:35
3 John 12:32
4 John 4:24
5 Philippians 1:6

Thank You, Father, that You cared enough for us to lead us to this place to grow. Thank You that You removed the attitude of "weirdness" that initially burdened us. Thank You that You take us to these exciting places as a family. What an incredible miracle and treasure it is to make this journey together.

"Imitate me, just as I also imitate Christ" (1 Corinthians 11:1).

PART 2

Gift-Wrapped Treasures

And this will be the sign to you: You will find a Babe
wrapped in swaddling cloths, lying in a manger.
—Luke 2:12

CHAPTER 6

Light

Arise, shine;
For your light has come!
And the glory of the LORD is risen upon you.
For behold, the darkness shall cover the earth,
And deep darkness the people;
But the LORD will arise over you,
And His glory will be seen upon you.[1]

I love Christmas. I have been known to leave my nativity up all year round to remind myself of all that Christ has done for me. He left His perfect home in heaven to come to be with me and to become like me, to enter into my human condition so He could identify with me.[2] I matter to Him. I am, in my humanity, powerless to follow Him as He desires. He invites me to come to Him, as I am, to learn and experience the unfathomable depths of His character.

By His grace and by His Spirit that He has given me, He leads me in His truth.[3] My part is to faithfully read His Word and intentionally commit my way to follow Him every single day. My faith and intentionality wane so they need to be renewed daily. For me to

---

[1] Isaiah 60:1–2
[2] Hebrews 4:15
[3] John 16:13

be His disciple, I not only need to know what He expects but I also need to commit in my heart and mind to make it my rule of conduct and allow it to change me.

As my mind is renewed with His truth,[4] He faithfully gives me the ability to be rescued from the lures of my flesh,[5] the deception of my heart,[6] and the indulgent culture around me. In His mercy, He keeps no record of my wrongs,[7] and He does not punish me as I deserve.[8] When I stray, He gives me yet another second chance to come clean before Him and to be healed. All my chances are second chances because He never remembers what I ask Him to forgive.[9]

This is the light that has come. His light shows me the way to my purpose and His peace in my life. It illuminates the deep darkness around me where I continually stumble and fall. Little by little, as I have chosen to know and follow Him, He has shown me more and more of His light. It is a continual and progressive process, building day after day. When I show up, He shows the way. When I doubt, He confirms His promises and truth to me. When I am overcome with sadness, He comforts me with His Word, perfectly illuminated at the perfect time without fail. It may not always be in my desired timing, but it is always without fail, building my faith and trust in Him along the way.

Let's take a closer and updated look at the Christmas story. The book of Luke gives us the most detailed account of the birth of Jesus. Luke was not a theologian. He was a doctor. He researched his SOAP note very carefully. He recorded what he heard (subjective), what he saw (objective), what it meant (assessment), and how it changed his life (plan). Why? So that we would have certainty of the truth.[10] The word *certainty* in the Greek is *asphaleia*,[11] meaning firmness or

---

4   Romans 12:2
5   1 John 2:16
6   Jeremiah 17:9
7   1 Corinthians 13:5
8   Psalm 103:10
9   Jeremiah 31:34
10   Luke 1:4
11   Strong's concordance #803, ASHPALEIA

security. If you have ever hit the asphalt, you know the firmness and certainty of it! That's enough to cause me to take a closer look at the truth born in a manger into a world of deception and full of fake news. The Bible is our ultimate fact-checker. If you fall for something less reliable, that's your own asphalt! (Read that as you will.) Luke intended that we be certain of the truth.

First of all, there were angels. These are not chubby, little, cherubic beings flying around with a bow and arrow igniting romance. No, these have been described by some as human telephone poles armed with swords. They do not inspire a cute little "ahh." Rather, they inspire a terrifying awe! The sword they wield is the Word of God, as they are His messengers.[12] In the Christmas story, the angel appeared to Zacharias, Mary, and Joseph. God's plan was made clear to each one. To each one, the angel declared, "Do not be afraid."[13] Then the angel would proceed with "Dude, this is the plan." Each one reacted differently.

Zacharias and Elizabeth had waited for and prayed for a child their whole life.[14] They were from a long line of temple priests, but that did not give them an advantage to answered prayer. They were both elderly and remained childless. In that day, to be childless was considered a disappointing and shameful thing. There was no one to carry on the family name and no one to be there to help as they aged. Children were, and still are, considered a heritage of the Lord, a reward from God.[15] Their lack of reward from God did not hinder them from serving in the temple. In fact, they are described as "blameless."[16] They were likely not perfect but they both possessed a real love and devotion to God despite their childlessness.

I wonder if Elizabeth and Zacharias ever stopped praying for a child. I wonder how many babies they had seen brought to the temple for dedication while their arms remained empty and their prayer unanswered. It's obvious that they didn't let confusion and

---

[12] Hebrews 1:14
[13] Luke 1:13; 1:30; Matthew 1:20
[14] Luke 1:13
[15] Psalm 127:3–5
[16] Luke 1:6

disappointment disrupt their obedience in serving. I wonder if they ever lost hope. Hope is not waiting for what we deserve or expect. It is looking forward to exceedingly, abundantly above all we can ask or imagine.[17] One of my favorite Scriptures offers this hope. "For the eyes of the Lord run to and fro throughout the whole earth to show Himself strong in behalf of those whose hearts are blameless toward Him."[18] That was Elizabeth and Zacharias. In the fullness of God's perfect time, not their time, their hope was realized. Though they had prayed for this for so long, it still came as a shock, seeming impossible.

Zacharias was not merely serving in the temple on the day the angel visited. It was his turn to burn incense before the Lord, a rare and serious responsibility. So in addition to the significant weight of his task, he also was greeted by the angel, promising him a child!

Zacharias questioned the angel. The angel answered, "I have come straight from God with the words and promise of God and you don't believe me? Okay. Now your mouth will be shut until it all comes to pass because if you keep talking like that, you will screw it all up!"[19] Sometimes God needs to shut our mouth while He does His best work. It may not look good at the onset, but God will be glorified in the outcome. In the fullness of time and in her advanced age, Elizabeth brought forth John the Baptist. I wonder if this event is the reason there are rocking chairs in nursing homes; nothing is impossible with God!

Matthew gives a shorter account of the birth of Christ, and he includes Joseph.[20] Joseph had a plan for his life that was just beginning to unfold before him. Joseph and Mary were betrothed. In Jewish culture, to be betrothed was as good as being married without the consummation. Betrothal was a binding contract, a covenant to be faithfully kept. The betrothal period was the time for the husband to build a room onto his father's house for himself and his bride. It is symbolic of our Father's house having many rooms and Jesus return-

[17] Ephesians 3:20
[18] 2 Chronicles 16:9
[19] Luke 1:20 (Rickson paraphrase)
[20] Matthew 1:18

ing for us, His bride. There is more on that in another chapter. So if I were Joseph, I would be in task mode. I would know what had to be done and how to do it. I would be a man on a mission. But then the angel showed up. According to Scripture, Joseph was from the line of David. Being a man of God, Joseph would have known that the Messiah would come from his "line."[21] But now? From him?

Matthew makes it very clear that Jesus would be Joseph's legal son but not his physical offspring. In fact, while Matthew is listing all the "begetting,"[22] Joseph is listed as Mary's husband,[23] not the father of Jesus. The angel addresses Joseph as the son of David, which may have been a clue to the news he was bringing. I wonder what thoughts ran through Joseph's heart and mind. Being more trusting than me, he likely didn't run through the list of excuses that come to my mind. But I am building a house. We are planning a wedding and a future together. We have not even been together. We have a reputation to uphold. Who will ever believe that this child is conceived of the Holy Spirit? Could *mine* be the house through which Messiah would come? How can I ever be a father to a Child Who will call Someone else Father?

Joseph did consider altering God's plan when he considered divorcing Mary secretly.[24] He was justified on the grounds of infidelity since she was pregnant. Their betrothal was legally binding. He could not simply walk away and wish Mary a good life. He did, however, have a choice to divorce her publicly or to keep it private between two witnesses.[25] Being a just man. Joseph wanted to do what was right in the eyes of God, not what would soothe his spirit or look good in the eyes of man. The angel confirmed to him that he should proceed with his betrothal because God was going to use them mightily. No, this was not the future that Joseph had envisioned. He was young and inexperienced, yet he was teachable and

---

[21] Isaiah 7:13
[22] Matthew 1:1–16
[23] Matthew 1:16
[24] Matthew 1:19
[25] Matthew 1:19

obedient. He allowed God to break in and change his plans as well as change the course of history!

Then there is Mary. She was pretty much the headliner of the story and the one who appeared the most compliant. She did start out troubled and confused[26] when the angel visited her, and his explanation made it even more baffling. She could not lean on her own understanding because there was no precedent for what she was about to experience. Who would ever believe that the child she was carrying was not the child of a man but of the Holy Spirit? That was a whopper no matter how spiritually mature you are, and she was a young girl. She had to face Joseph, her parents, her rabbi, her synagogue friends, the judgy neighbors, and her future. The angel, however, said she was blessed and highly favored because she had a God Who was with her and in her. Mary had to be completely and totally reliance on His Word. She had to proceed in humility and trusting obedience to bring God's plan to full gestation. We know how the story ends, but she had to walk it out in faith. Have you ever been there? It may look like blind faith, but Mary had her eyes riveted on her God.

Mary was a perfect example of this Scripture: "The people who *know*[27] (intimately) their God shall be strong & carry out great exploits."[28] Mary magnified[29] what she *knew* over what she didn't know. She may have known little, but it was enough in the hands of her God. The innkeeper may have turned the holy family away on the night of Jesus's birth, but Mary and Joseph made ample room for the Son of God in their lives so that He could birth His perfect plan through them.

Scripture tells us to let our light shine before men that they may see our good works and glorify our Father in heaven.[30] His light in me is not to illuminate myself. It is to illuminate Him, to put the spotlight on Him, the source of all light. I do not have inherent

---

[26] Luke 1:29
[27] Strong's concordance #3045, YADA
[28] Daniel 11:32
[29] Luke 1:46
[30] Matthew 5:16

light. I reflect His light. Just as the moon cannot shine without the sun, I have nothing to show off without Him. He is the Light of the world.[31] When I try to shine my own light, I lead myself astray. I follow the wrong path and find myself lost in the darkness without direction. I shine the light on my inadequacy rather than His sufficiency. When I try to run out ahead of His light, I can find myself shipwrecked. He may give me only enough light for the place He intends me to be. Mary and Joseph did not have a blueprint for the entire plan. They were obedient to the Light that they had at the moment. They were not interested in shining their own light. They completely abandoned their immediate plans to bring forth the light in the darkness and the Savior in the silence that they had known for four hundred years.

The Light has come. God did not shine from afar. He came down to us. The light of the world arrived that night. He didn't just send a messenger, a letter, an email or a text. He revealed Himself. God showed up in person so we could know Him. His arrival was announced to ordinary people working the night shift. These were shepherds watching their flocks.[32] Shepherds were the often-forgotten working class. Remember how David was overlooked by his father when Samuel came to anoint the next king of Israel?[33] But it was the shepherds, not the elite of society, who were given the breaking news of the holy birth. The angel appeared to them as well and had to put their fears to rest. They chose to go and see for themselves. What did they find? Divinity in human form Who split time forever from BC to AD. Love personified, light in darkness, hope in despair, joy in sorrow, peace in chaos, forgiveness in offense, wisdom in confusion. He still calls us today to "Come and see."[34] We cannot, however, leave Christ in the manger. There is so much more of Him!

We must look at Christmas through a wide-angle lens. This world is like Motel 6. He left the light on for us, but this is not our final destination. We are not made for this place because He has

---

[31] John 8:12
[32] Luke 2:8
[33] 1 Samuel 16:11
[34] John 1:30

made a place for us.[35] When the fullness of time comes, He will complete time and we will step into eternity. Our eternity will either be with Him or apart from Him. The choice is ours. The manger is a signpost,[36] not the destination. It leads us home.

Though we are surrounded by deep darkness, we can know His light through His Holy Spirit dwelling within us. It is not to illuminate ourselves but to show His glory and His light to others who need His direction. My life has been a continual journey of stumbling in the darkness and being rescued by His light. I may not know the entire plan He has for me, but I must be willing to set aside my plans for His plans. It is not in blind faith but in trusting reliance because of Who He has shown Himself to be for me. I may question Him. I may be troubled and confused. I may be wandering around minding my own business when He interrupts my plans. But of one thing, I am sure. If I follow Him, I will never be left in darkness. He will lead me home with Him. For that, I am grateful.

Lord Jesus, thank You for the light that You have brought to our deep darkness. Thank You for the light of Your grace toward us, ordinary people in our ordinary lives…until we see YOU! Thank you that, as we look to You, Your glory is seen in and through us. The light of Your grace and glory. It's the gift that keeps on giving!

"Let it be to me according to YOUR WORD" (Luke 1:38).

---

[35] John 14:2
[36] Luke 2:12

CHAPTER 7

Wait... What?

The spiritual preparation for Christmas begins with Advent. Advent is a time of expectation and anticipation, preparing us for the arrival of our King. We saw in the last chapter how God used His people in unexpected ways to bring forth His perfect plan. When the fullness of time had come, God sent forth His Son.[1] The Father said it's time! There had been no word from God for four hundred years. The prophets had been silent. Unexpectedly and suddenly angels burst forth to disrupt lives. Though it had been prophesied for centuries, no one expected what was about to happen now that time had been fulfilled.

We know that God's people expected a warrior to come to free them from the Roman oppression. Elizabeth and Zacharias expected to live out their days childless. Mary and Joseph's life together was just beginning. Everyone's expectations were upended.

Elizabeth had hoped for a child all her life. In her culture, barrenness was a cause for shame. Elizabeth had likely expected a life of reproach[2] forever. Wait. What? Mary was a teenage virgin, bearing the shame of an unwed pregnancy. She likely expected to be shunned as a sinner and her betrothal to Joseph broken. Wait. What? God, as He so often does, used both of them and their shame. In fact, He used it for His glory! Those are some great expectations that arose

---

[1]   Galatians 4:4
[2]   Luke 1:25

from the pit of shame. But neither Elizabeth nor Mary had read the end of the story when they were cast in it. They needed to walk it out by faith, as do we, often leaving us questioning. Wait. What?

If we are troubled and confused, can God still use us? (Asking for a friend!) When the angel Gabriel spoke to Mary, she was troubled and confused.[3] The word for *troubled* in the Greek means to be "greatly agitated, acutely distressed."[4] Can you relate? Based on Scripture, it seems that Mary transitioned very quickly to submitting to the Word of God. She set aside her own expectations and declared, "Behold the maidservant of the Lord! Let it be to me according to Your word."[5] She then went to visit Elizabeth, who was on a similarly unexpected path.

Mary magnified her Lord in the middle of their upended expectations, remembering the covenant that God had made with Abraham and his descendants.[6] She didn't understand what was happening, but she knew what God had done in the past and that was enough for her. She knew the Word of God and the God of the Word. Mary understood covenant. In our culture, we have lost the true meaning of covenant. But God remembers. What He has promised, He *will* deliver, no matter how upended our plans become. Though Mary was not certain of how the story would end, she chose to plant her hope in the covenant and all that God had promised to her and her people. She trusted Him no matter what it looked like from her perspective.

God was looking for someone to bring forth His Son. He was not looking for someone with talent, position, experience, reputation, riches, or perfection. He was looking for someone with trust. He was looking for a place where He could grow unhindered, unassisted, and unresisted. Someone in whom He could live until He could be delivered into the world. God had walked *with* Adam and Eve, Abraham, Moses, David, and the disciples; but He had never walked *in* anyone before now. Jesus came to show us a whole new way. He was conceived in Mary to show how He wants to live in us. What a treasure!

---

3 Luke 1:29
4 Strong's concordance #1298, DIATARRASSO
5 Luke 1:38
6 Luke 1:55

When my plans are upended, I often forget what He has promised me and I become, like Mary, troubled, agitated, and distressed. If I don't reorient myself to the truth, I can remain in that state for a long time. As a recovering control freak, I have had many opportunities to practice setting aside my own expectations. Mary did and she brought forth the Savior, not only of her own people but the Savior of the world. Many of the Jews did not set aside their own expectations of a Warrior Savior, and they missed the Sacrificial Lamb Who came to bring them so much more than political freedom. We can often be very short-sighted and miss the abundance that He intends for us.

In the uncertainty of this world, we cannot lose sight of the certainty of God's promises and the covenant He has made with those who choose Jesus. His covenant with us is for eternity, eternal life. To God, eternal life is not life in the hereafter. It is, rather, to intimately know the Father, right now, thru Jesus[7] here on planet earth in the midst of our upended plans and expectations. It has been said that eternal life is not pie in the sky by and by when you die but steak on our plate as you wait![8]

Thankfully, His covenant is not based on my wavering belief but on the certainty of His character. Even in my trouble and confusion, He has promised,

> If we are faithless,
> He remains faithful;
> He cannot deny Himself.[9]

I personally had a plan when our three oldest daughters were preteens. In response to our pastor's challenge to get out of our holy huddle and make a difference in the world, I chose to run for our local school board. I had been actively involved in our local schools for years with my children and had many to support and encourage me. I was confident in my ability to serve, my motivation for that

---

[7] John 17:3
[8] Source unknown
[9] 2 Timothy 2:13

service and in my God. I "knew" where He was leading me, and I was happy to follow. I was obeying His command to be a "light in the world"[10] shining in the darkness. My candidacy required that I participate in a public forum with the five other candidates. This was miles out of my comfort zone, but God's grace prevailed. I was sure that this was His calling for me.

The day of the election came. I lost by seven votes. Wait. What? My dignity was somewhat preserved as I had come really close to winning but I was confused, troubled, and agitated. I thought I knew where we were going. Now I found myself in the darkness. After my head stopped spinning and my mind stopped asking, I settled back into life as it had been, still wondering how I could have missed my call. But all the time I was planning to do something for God, He had planned something for me to do!

A few weeks later, as I was back in my life as a NICU nurse, I was introduced to a two-and-a-half-pound baby girl, born eleven weeks prematurely. She had been surprisingly healthy despite her prematurity but was diagnosed with feeding intolerance and failure to thrive. The nursery was very busy at the time of her birth, so there had been no time for holding and feeding and comforting babies. We were all in task mode, prioritizing the most vital activities with each baby. This baby's parents had their own challenges, so visiting and bonding opportunities were limited. Because she was mostly fed by intravenous nutrition, her human contact was very limited, thus contributing to her failure to thrive. It was a vicious cycle. Her feeding intolerance caused her to spend months in the nursery under these conditions.

I was "visiting" her through her incubator one evening when my friend and colleague, Phyllis, joined me. I had worked with Phyllis for a long while, and she knew our family well. Without much thought, I mused that we could give this baby a good home. She immediately responded, "Why don't you?"

Wait! What? We were not looking to have any more children, the children we had were well on their way to independence, my life was full of all kinds of activities, and we were comfortable right where

---

[10] Philippians 2:15

we were. I had a laundry list of excuses. Then "the angel" stepped in and said, "Don't be afraid."[11] I love a good challenge, so my thoughts turned to a new mission. It was to take this baby home temporarily and prove what some tender loving care could do for a baby unable to grow. It would be continuity of care at its best. When I first talked it over with my husband, Ernie, he was all in. My daughters were excited as well. We all knew that this would be a temporary situation, in which this baby could be returned to her birth mother, but we were willing to love and care for her for the time being.

The process of being educated and licensed for foster care began. We gathered up baby supplies, which we had gotten rid of years earlier. I applied for a leave from my work in the NICU. We worked to reunite the birth family by providing daily visits and parenting education and support, but reunification was not possible in the end. Even so, that beautiful baby grew and thrived. Her social skills were severely limited when we first took her home from the hospital at three months of age. When first home, she was unable to maintain eye contact and was very easily over stimulated. This was a picture taken on the day she came home.

(The object you see in the background is a coin bank and not the bottle we would use to feed her!)

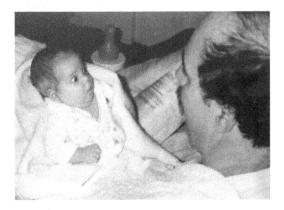

---

[11]   Luke 1:13, 1:30; Matthew 1:20

Little by little, she became very social and the center of attention. She grew way beyond her initial limitations and our limited expectations.

We experienced eighteen months of uncertainty, not knowing if she would remain in our family or be reunited with her birth mother. We had gone into this endeavor as a temporary situation, but circumstances kept pointing to a possibly different outcome. It required that we do what we had been called to do, one day and one step at a time.

Stormie Omartian describes it as "having just enough light for the step I'm on." After eighteen months, Jenna did, indeed, become part of our family forever. She has been a cherished and chosen part of our family for over thirty years now. It was not my plan in my limited vision, but God clearly had a plan for all of us. We actually have two cherished and chosen ones in our family. The story of our second chosen one, Caitlin, is clearly veiled in deep darkness to be revealed in another chapter. Just as an aside, my friend Phyllis also became the proud mother of two beautiful and very fortunate adopted children. God never ceases to amaze us!

How often do I think I know what God's best plan is for me? How often do I advise Him and run ahead of His plan straight into the darkness? Looking back, the disappointment of losing the school board election paled in comparison to the joy that God had intended for me in becoming a mother again. A few years earlier, we had decided not to have any more birth children for a number of reasons. I had always secretly wished that that permanent decision would fail. We, however, hadn't taken any precautions against adoption! What a treasured surprise.

It is certainly not my intention to compare myself to Elizabeth bearing John the Baptist or to Mary bearing the Son of God. But again, "for the eyes of the LORD run to and fro throughout the whole earth, to show Himself strong on behalf of those whose heart is loyal to Him."[12]

His search is not for the rich and famous or the bold and the beautiful. He is looking for a loyal heart. Not a perfect heart but one who desires to be His and who is willing to trust Him for the plan

---

[12] 2 Chronicles 16:9

and the outcome. My trust may have been fragmented and questioning at times, but it was enough for Him to be able to work His plan over mine.

By His death and resurrection, Christ has placed His Spirit within us. He no longer walks with us but is within us, as close as He can be. He desires that His Spirit grow unhindered and unresisted in us so that we can deliver Christ and His light into a world of deafening silence about the truth and thick darkness.[13] He desires to be "Christ in you, the hope of glory."[14]

His love is so much higher, wider, purer, and wiser than ours, looking beyond who we are to who we can be in Him. How the endless limits of His love fit into a human Baby is beyond me. But make no mistake. It did!

Lord, thank You that you don't require perfection but that you are looking for willingness. You take our confusion and weave it into Your perfect plan, if we allow. You know the end from the beginning, and You can be trusted. All my own agenda and expectations aside, my prayer is that You will use me to bring Your light and freedom to those who need it.

I make known the end from the beginning,
from ancient times, what is still to come.
I say, "My purpose will stand, and I will do
all that I please." (Isaiah 46:10)

Afternote: Jenna's social skills advanced to the point where, as a preschooler, she stood at the top of a stairway overlooking a crowded beach and exclaimed excitedly, "Look! All my friends are here!" It was not uncommon for her to be included in other family's vacation photos because of her charm. She certainly portrayed what He means by exceedingly, abundantly above all we ask or think.[15]

---

[13] Isaiah 60:2
[14] Colossians 1:27
[15] Ephesians 3:20

CHAPTER 8

Anna

Anna was a woman of hope and expectation. She gets introduced after the Christmas story. She knew how to wait. We see her cameo in Luke 2:36–38, three short verses packed with significance. Introduced as the daughter of Phanuel, her rich heritage points back to Genesis 32:30 where Jacob wrestled with God and saw Him face-to-face. Jacob named that place Penuel, the Hebrew origin of the name Phanuel. *Penuel* means "face of God." Keep that in mind as we go on.

Anna was a widow from a young age and remained that way to her dying day. In Anna's day, being a widow meant being vulnerable, without provision or protection. Perhaps that's why she did not depart from the temple. I wonder what it was like in the temple. Was it a solemn gathering, focused on the rituals or was it a place of joy in His presence? Scripture clearly says that there is fullness of joy in His presence and pleasures forevermore.[1] Do you suppose Anna ever wrestled with her earthly lot or did the joy of her environment overshadow that?

She is also identified as being a descendant of the tribe of Asher, one of the twelve tribes of Israel. Anna had a heritage that promised God's best for her as one of His chosen people. Do you suppose that she saw her widowhood as God's best for her? As a long-time widow, I

---

[1]   Psalm 16:11

46

have struggled with that very question. Is this how His chosen people exist? Is this His favor? Didn't He say at the very beginning that it is not good that man should be alone?[2] That is my own private wrestling match, but it apparently did not cause Anna to lose hope and confident expectation. She continued faithfully waiting and serving in the temple with her neck stretched out looking expectantly for what her God had ahead.

Anna was identified as a prophetess at a time when there were no prophets speaking for God. Anna was the chosen one who "spoke of Him to all those who looked for redemption in Jerusalem."[3] Even in the silence, Anna was driven by her trust in her faithful God. She didn't allow the silence or the pain of her past to interfere with her purpose for the days ahead. In her confident, undaunted expectation, she continued to look around the corner, anticipating the new mercies of her God every morning. Anna was empowered to revive the spirit of prophecy that had been dormant for four hundred years. She didn't seem to doubt it, criticize it, or analyze it. She didn't need to understand it or try to make it fit into her theological box. She gave God full access to speak freely and be fully expressed through her, against all odds, without wavering.

Anna was present in the temple when Mary and Joseph brought Jesus to the temple when He was just over a month old. His parents brought Him to "present Him to the Lord"[4] and to offer a sacrifice according to the Law. So the Lord was presented to the Lord according to Himself, the Word. Chew on that for a while! Anyway, Anna waited and served in the temple for decades before she was able to see the face of God (remember Penuel?) in Jesus the Messiah. The only thing she knew to do was to do what waiters do, serve.

In spite of her circumstances, Anna didn't forget her God-given heritage as a daughter of the King. She remembered that she came from a long line of being "in the face of God." Her heritage and her legacy seemed to be important to her. Scripture doesn't say if she had

---

[2] Genesis 2:18
[3] Luke 2:38
[4] Luke 2:22

birth children, but it is likely that she had multitudes of spiritual children, given the years she spent in the temple in the presence of God. Anna didn't look back at all she had lost. She seemed focused on what God had for her in her future. She did not seem to squander her life staring in the rearview mirror and so miss the Glory before her very eyes. She never lost sight of the treasure that was waiting for her ahead, and she indeed saw God face-to-face.

Anna's name means "grace." She was likely not a grumpy old woman scolding children for running in the inner court, wanting to share her misery. I see her as a wise and gracious woman, teaching others reverence and fear of the Lord and respect for the things of God. Because of her devotion to her God, her heart was pure, and her spirit was gentle.[5] She is the quintessential Proverbs 31 woman despite her circumstances. Her deeds spoke for themselves. She was able and willing to extend grace to others because she was aware of the abundance of grace extended to her by her God. She feared and praised the Lord, and she apparently desired the same for others as she did not keep the discovery of her Messiah to herself but spoke freely of Him.[6]

I wonder if she was ever envious of those who have been blessed with what she may have desired. She must have grieved the loss of her husband, her dreams, and her plans for the future. After all, she was human. But we don't see her throwing a pity party or riding the woe-is-me train. We do, however, see her celebrating how God had chosen to uniquely use her, bless her, and favor her as she stared into the face of her Messiah. This sight was likely exceedingly, abundantly above all she could have asked or imagined![7] She was blessed in a unique way, a way unknown to others who went about their everyday life and missed the treasure that awaited Anna in her obedience.

She didn't seem to allow her advanced age to give her an excuse to rest. Her attitude was not "I've put in my time and given it my all." She didn't sit back and let others pray and fast and attend to the tem-

---

[5]   1 Peter 3:4
[6]   Luke 2:38
[7]   Ephesians 3:20

ple. She gave herself wholly to the work of the Lord. Maybe she was tired, but she remained steadfast. She wanted to be sure she would not be benched in her advanced age. She seemed to know there was more. She was confident that there was something or Someone worth the wait and the work.

Scripture tells us to "work out your own salvation with fear and trembling."[8] I cannot work out your salvation, and you cannot work out mine. We each have our own unique assignment. The work for "work out" in the Greek is *katergazomai*.[9] It means to bring to a decisive conclusion or to work to an end point. It carries the context of digging the silver out of a silver mine.[10] The treasure that was hidden deep in Anna needed to be mined through decades of waiting, serving and hoping.

Anna's service in the temple didn't seem to be out of guilt or obligation. She was likely not serving out of resentment as a martyr for the way her life had turned out or for the acknowledgment of man. All those things run out of steam before the end of the race. She served God "day and night"[11] for His honor, not her own. She worked with fear and trembling. Her fear was not one of dread or being afraid of God. Her fear was out of respect and honor for the God she knew. Her continual fasting and prayer day and night were driven by her fear of displeasing the One she loved and to Whom she was devoted. Her service was not to be noticed by others but so that she could notice the One sent for her redemption. She worked to please only One.

In keeping with her Proverbs 31 character, she didn't let worldly concerns distract her from her mission. She was exactly where she needed to be "in that instant."[12] She did not miss the moment for which she had been called and for which she had waited. She didn't seem caught up in the culture outside the temple or in the hope of finding a new husband as a means out of her present state. She didn't

---

[8] Philippians 2:12 NKJV
[9] Strong's concordance #2716, KATERGAZOMAI
[10] Nelson's NKJV Study Bible, Luke 2:12 study note
[11] Luke 2:37
[12] Luke 2:38

seem interested in providing a life for herself apart from God. She was kingdom-minded, and she was rewarded by seeing His kingdom come in the flesh.

Scripture doesn't say that she grumbled and complained about her circumstances as was the habit of her ancient predecessors.[13] She didn't appear to feel cheated or regret having missed out on the what others may have considered the fullness of life. She appeared full of anticipation for what God would do for her in her present day, never losing sight of her promised Messiah. Her words were full of hope as she tells *all*[14] of her Savior and His promised redemption. With no fear of ridicule or of looking foolish, she declared what God had revealed to her. She did not have to keep the mystery to herself. She knew her God. She knew what He had promise, and He had confirmed His promise to her. Her God had freely given her a glimpse onto His mystery, and she shared her testimony with all who would listen. She could speak boldly and confidently.

She wouldn't have let petty differences with others derail her from her purpose or cause her to withdraw or turn away from God. She didn't seem to need to protect or defend herself or her God. God defended her by allowing her to see Himself face-to-face. She did not need to be easily offended because she knew who she was and to Whom she belonged. Her heart was undivided. Her focus and purpose were devoted to pleasing her God and no one else. She knew what He had promised. She knew the joy of obedience and she joyfully delivered. She could freely celebrate the long-awaited Messiah because of the hope to which she had so tightly held. This was the hope that changed her from an empty and vulnerable woman to one who could praise and be praised.

When she finally could look into the face of her Savior, she must have known it was all worth it. She could offer her worship, declaring the worth-ship of the God Who had proven Himself faithful again and again. He had provided for her every need as a widow.

---

[13] 1 Corinthians 10:10
[14] Luke 2:38

She had learned to be at peace and content with her earthly lot. I love how the Amplified Bible translates it:

> And God's peace [shall be yours, that tranquil state of a soul assured of its salvation through Christ, and so fearing nothing from God and being content with its earthly lot of whatever sort that is, that peace] which transcends all understanding shall garrison and mount guard over your hearts and minds in Christ Jesus.[15]

Now she is thankful[16] that her circumstances have allowed her to be free to serve Him day and night without other obligations, allowing her to see the Messiah, her salvation. It was worth the waiting and the hoping beyond hope.[17] She anticipated expectantly, free from her own limiting expectations. Being kingdom-minded, she kept eternity in her heart[18] so the temporal had no effect on her. Being secure in her identity as a child of the Father, she persevered and did not miss the moment for which she had been destined. Finally, the fulfillment of the promise was in her sight. The search had not been in vain. The Promise had been revealed and she didn't miss it. She saw and gave light to the abundant grace of God in Jesus the Messiah.

Lord, let me be like Anna. Let me fear nothing except displeasing You.

"The secret things belong to the LORD our God, but those things which are revealed belong to us and to our children forever, that we may do all the words of this law" (Deuteronomy 29:29).

---

[15] Philippians 4:7 AMPC
[16] Luke 2:38
[17] Romans 4:18
[18] Ecclesiastes 3:11

CHAPTER 9

Traditions

Who doesn't love Santa? Like a good father, he invites us up on his lap. We see his welcoming smile. We hear his voice speaking our name. He listens as we pour out the desires of our hearts. He gives gifts and he also has expectations if we are to avoid the naughty list. It is only children who don't know him or understand his mission who fear him.

Jesus came to be the star of Christmas so why do we let Him take a back seat? Why do we allow a childhood character to overshadow our Savior? Jesus reveals the perfect Father. He is the exact representation of Who God is.[1] Jesus came to tell us all that the Father wants to say to us.[2] He calls us to come near to Him.[3] He draws us close on His lap. He knows and calls us by our name[4] without anyone telling Him. He bends down to hear us[5] when we speak to Him. He welcomes our hopes and our dreams and gives the best gifts.[6] His gifts will not wear out by New Year's Day. In fact, they last into eternity. Jesus's only expectation is that we receive Him, that we believe He is Who He says He is and follow Him. Do we know

---

[1] Hebrews 1:3
[2] John 12:49
[3] James 4:8
[4] Isaiah 43:1
[5] Psalm 116:2
[6] James 1:17

Him? Do we understand His mission? Do we fear Him or fear being in His disfavor?

The more we get to know Him, the more we desire to know Him. The more we know Him, the more we want to spend time with Him. We don't have to travel to the mall during limited hours. We don't have to make an appointment to see Him. We don't even have to wait in line to spend time with Him. He is always available at the call of His Name. He is ever-present and always listening. It is we who need to tune into Him because His ears are always open to us. We are the ones who suffer from auditory processing disorder. It is difficult to hear Him and understand what He is saying and follow His directions in this noisy place we call the world. It requires practice and intention to be able to tune out background noise and focus on Him.

Santa can't empower us to avoid the naughty list, but Jesus can.[7] Santa shows up in December and elusively disappears by the end of the year. Jesus is Immanuel, God with us. He is with us always and will never leave us.[8] What a promise to treasure!

Do we really understand the meaning of our traditions? Do we understand the reason behind the nativity that we display so proudly? In our manger scenes, Baby Jesus is wrapped in swaddling cloths. Some say that those cloths were scraps of old priestly garments that were set aside to reused as wicks for the temple lamps that burned continually night and day.[9] Remember that Zacharias was serving as priest when he was promised a son.[10] Perhaps the swaddling cloths were a gift from Elizabeth and Zacharias when Mary visited Elizabeth in celebration of their unexpected pregnancies.

Temple shepherds also commonly used the cloths to protect newborn lambs from defect and injury. These lambs were specifically bred and set aside to be used for temple sacrifices for sin. They had to be spotless, according to the Law.[11] It was the temple shepherd's

[7] Philippians 2:13
[8] Deuteronomy 31:8
[9] Exodus 27:20
[10] Luke 1:8
[11] Leviticus 22:19

task to ensure that they were not bruised as they wobbled around on newborn legs.

So in this scenario, we see Jesus in the light, the spotless Lamb, the Good Shepherd and our Great High Priest, offering forgiveness of sin. God never wastes anything!

Giving is the way of Christmas. Immanuel came at Christmas, but He didn't leave when the last gift was opened. He brought the gift of His love and gave His love as an assignment for us. His love is our gift to receive and our mission to give. His assignment is still relevant today. Simply put, it is to "Love one another like it's Me."[12] We are called to serve one another, from the least to the greatest. Each one of us is created in His image and we have been charged with housing His Spirit.[13] We are the package in which His most precious gift is wrapped. The apostle Paul says it like this: "But we have this treasure in earthen vessels, that the excellence of the power may be of God and not of us."[14]

We are all cracked pots into which God pours the Spirit of His Son when we agree to receive Him. Our job is to deliver Jesus to the world. We are all created in the image of God. If we really looked for and were able to see Jesus in each other, from the greatest to the least, would we act differently? If we saw each other equally as each one in desperate need of a Savior, would we have more compassion? Even the rich and famous and powerful have the same desperate need as those in deep financial and social need. One of the greatest gifts we could receive is new eyes to see Him in everyone that He has created. We need eyes to see Him in the kind and in the grumpy, in the hurried and the distracted, in the affluent and in the needy, in the cute and the messy. We all bear the fingerprints of our Creator. That, Charlie Brown, is what Christ came to teach us when He stooped down and entered our world.

We do love the gifts, though. Receiving a gift thoughtfully given brings us great joy. It may be the preschool handprints of our

---

[12]   Matthew 25:40
[13]   1 Corinthians 6:19
[14]   2 Corinthians 4:7

children. It may be a card written with heartfelt gratitude and love. It is something that communicates that we are valuable to the giver.

There is also great joy in giving a gift. The greatest of gifts from the giver are things someone really needs or earnestly desires. It may be something that they can't obtain on their own or would not consider buying for themselves. It is probably something that they will "use" every day. It may be the gift of time or service. It is something that will constantly remind the recipient that they are loved and valued.

God came to our broken world in a manger to show us that we are loved and valued. He came to bring us the gift of joy. The psalmist David said it like this: "In Your Presence is fullness of joy."[15]

God graced us with His presence in Jesus. He showed us His favor by leaving the glories of heaven and coming to the squalor of earth. He clothed Himself in human flesh so we could see him, so we could hear Him, so He could be touched and followed. It is the presence of Jesus that gives us genuine joy. The Greek word for joy is *chara*.[16] It means the gladness that comes because of the awareness of God's grace. The Greek word for grace is *charis*.[17] Grace is the complete and freely expressed favor and loving kindness of God to us. It is unconditional and springs only from the benevolence and goodness of our loving God. It is not dependent on our success or failure. It cannot be earned. It is freely given. God showed His grace to us by reaching out in the form of a Baby in a manger to bless us. Therein lies our joy!

Jesus came to bring us His joy, not as the world perceives joy. Joy is not the same as happiness. Happiness is often dependent on circumstances. Joy goes beyond our present condition. Scripture gives us this direction: "Looking unto Jesus, the author and finisher of our faith, Who for the joy that was set before Him endured the cross, despising the shame, and has sat down at the right hand of the throne of God."[18]

---

[15] Psalm 16:11
[16] Strong's concordance #5479, CHARA
[17] Strong's concordance #5485, CHARIS
[18] Hebrews 12:2

There is no joy visible in the cross unless we understand why Jesus endured it. He focused on His mission. He came in a manger to die on a cross so we could live with Him forever. He had to die as the spotless Lamb of God to satisfy the wrath of a holy God. God could not just ignore our sin inherited from Adam. He could not wink at our stains and invite us in. That would compromise His holiness. Jesus chose to die in our place to make us acceptable to the Father. Jesus's work restored our fellowship with our Holy God. Jesus opened the way to heaven. It is the only way.[19] Jesus saw beyond the cross to eternity. We can be clothed in the work of His righteousness, His shed blood on the cross, to cover our inborn sin and self-centeredness. As we receive the gift of Jesus, we become fit for heaven. Jesus chose to die for us, so He didn't have to live without us. That's love. That's grace. That's joy. That's the gift that God sent. God showed us His favor in the face of Christ so we could know joy. His joy is endless, unconditional, and eternal. It's for everyone. It's for me and you. Go ahead. Open it. And see *His* joy when you do!

Lord, Thank You for the priceless gift of Your presence wrapped in the flesh of an infant. Thank You for Your patience in waiting for me to open it. Forgive me for the times I have taken it for granted. Your gift of grace in Your presence is all I have ever really needed or desired. There are other things that may surface to try to take Your place, but in the end, You are all I need. You know the way. You are the way. You show the way to make it through this world to be with you for eternity.

"And this is eternal life, that they may know You, the only true God, and Jesus Christ whom You have sent" (John 17:3).

---

[19] John 14:6

CHAPTER 10

Betrothal

I am a hopeless romantic. One of the greatest joys of my life was to be a bride. Even on the days I was not particularly radiant or beautiful, my husband, Ernie, called me his bride. He knew it made my day and most often changed my mood for the better. The greatest sorrow of my life has been to lose the one on earth who called me his bride. You can read more about that in my first book, *A Walk Through the Shadow*.

The Jewish wedding is a beautiful expression of what God intends for His people. God chose to deliver His Son through Mary who was betrothed to Joseph.[1] In Jewish culture, marriage is a little different than what we know. The preparation for the wedding is the betrothal, which is divided into two parts. In the first part, the groom announces his intent to care for the bride. He presents a written marriage contract for the bride to accept. A ceremony is held under a wedding canopy where a blessing is pronounced over the couple. They each drink from a cup of wine and exchange rings, promising themselves to each other. The groom promises to take care of the bride and the bride promises to set herself apart for her groom. She becomes officially free from her parent's household but has to wait for the wedding to actually change her location.

---

[1] Luke 1:27

This begins their betrothal or engagement. A period of least a year will elapse before the actual wedding ceremony will be celebrated. This, however, is the beginning of the new covenant between them. The marriage contract or betrothal is as good as a wedding covenant. A certificate of divorce is required to void the contract, an option available only to the groom. (There is good news in relation to this later, so don't leave me now!)

According to the marriage contract, the couple is considered married, but they live separately, and there is no physical contact before the wedding day. The denial of physical contact is intentional so that they can be united in spirit before their bodies are united.[2] The purpose is to prevent their physical connection from overshadowing their spiritual connection, thus skewing the intention of marriage. Both the bride and groom prepare themselves to enter into the covenant of marriage.

The groom pays a bridal price to the bride's family, but it actually belongs to the bride. This payment officially changes her status to betrothed, set apart for him alone. During the year of their separation, the bridal price continually reminds the bride of her groom's pledge of love for her. It symbolizes his promise to return for her and take her to himself. The bride also presents her dowry, signifying that she is prepared to yield whatever she has to her husband and keep herself for him alone.

During that year, they both make preparations to celebrate their wedding covenant. The bride spends most the betrothal year preparing her wedding garment. The year is full of anticipation and excitement. The arrival of the groom is always anticipated but never expected. They never know the day or the hour when the groom will be released to come for his bride. The bride has to always be ready, watchful, and eagerly expecting his arrival.

During that year, the groom returns to his home to prepare a new dwelling for his bride and their future family. It is typically a room built on the groom's father's house. The expectation is that the new dwelling will be better than the place from which the bride

---

[2] Naftali Silberberg, *Kiddushin—Betrothal*. Chabad.org.

has come. This is determined by the groom's father. The room must meet the father's approval before the groom can bring his bride home. Only the groom's father knows when this will take place and it is solely his decision When the groom is released to receive his bride, the second phase of the betrothal ceremony is celebrated.

When the groom's father gives the final approval, the shofar is sounded, and the groom's party announces the groom's arrival at the bride's home. The groom will go for his bride and carry her to their new home. This ceremony also takes place under the wedding canopy where they finalize promises and vows. Their marriage is blessed, and the marriage supper can commence. This event is a week-long gathering with an abundance of food, wine, and celebration.

To look back at Scripture is to see God's plan to claim us, His church, as His bride.

First, we have His intent. God stated His intent in the very first chapters of Genesis. He created the perfect environment. He created the animals that would be needed for the covering for Adam and Eve when they fell even before they came on the earth. He created everything and called it all "good." Then He said, "Let Us make man in Our image, according to Our likeness."[3] All that God had already created was not sufficient for the fellowship that He intended. God's intention for man was fellowship, communion and union with Him.

Man was deceived into turning away from God through sin. God still, however, provided a way for that fellowship to be restored by animal sacrifices until the perfect substitutionary sacrifice for sin could come in Jesus Christ. God made continual covenants with us through Noah to Abraham to Moses and David. There was always a remnant of those who would stay in fellowship with God. Jesus ushered in the New Covenant with the same intention and commitment to betroth us to Himself.

Second, God has given us His marriage contract. God illustrates the faithfulness of His covenant through the prophet Hosea. God instructed Hosea to marry a prostitute named Gomer. The prostitute illustrates our unworthiness and unfaithfulness to God.

---

[3] Genesis 1:26

Hosea's pursuit of and faithfulness to Gomer despite her unfaithfulness illustrates God's relentless pursuit of us as His own. It is a picture of God's covenant to His beloved Israel and ultimately to us. God is committed to His covenant, and He desires for us to have a loyal and intimate relationship with Him. He is jealous[4] for our affection and will not stand for rivals to His affection. He has gone to great lengths to secure our relationship with Him and Hosea illustrates that as he repeatedly buys Gomer back off the slave block. The name Gomer is derived from the Hebrew word *gamar*, meaning perfect or complete.[5] I can clearly see the "*me*" in go*me*r. If God can perfect a stubborn, rebellious prostitute like her, then perhaps there is hope for me!

> I will betroth you to Me forever;
> Yes, I will betroth you to Me
> In righteousness and justice,
> In lovingkindness and mercy;
> I will betroth you to Me in faithfulness,
> And you shall know the Lord.[6]

Third, God desires us to know Him, in the most intimate, *yada*,[7] kind of way. This is the same intimacy with which a husband knows his wife. God desires that we be faithful to Him, set apart for Him and be with Him forever.

I do not take for granted the privilege I had of experiencing a wonderful love and marriage here on earth for thirty years and four days. It was not perfect, but I was blessed and changed by it. As the years have gone by since Ernie has been in heaven, I have found myself idealizing and idolizing that relationship. With each passing year that we are apart, the more perfect our relationship becomes in my remembrance. Even this blessing that God provided for me started becoming a stumbling block in my relationship with

---

4   Exodus 20:5
5   Strong's Concordance #1584, GAMAR
6   Hosea 2:19–20
7   Strong's Concordance #3045, YADA

God. Every good and perfect gift is from Him.[8] He intends that we love the gift but worship the Giver. I found myself idealizing what I remembered. It was becoming idol worship of what I had lost. But God is ever faithful, even when we are led astray. God continually works on me to "*gamar*" and perfect me according to His plan and purposes. He will not allow anything to come between the intimacy that He desires with me. For that, I am grateful.

Fourth, we have God's blessing. With God's intent for man being made clear, He continually pronounces a blessing on us by His Words throughout Scripture. One of my favorites is spoken through Moses:

> The LORD bless you and keep you;
> The LORD make His face shine upon you,
> And be gracious to you;
> The LORD lift up His countenance upon you,
> And give you peace.
> So they shall put My name on the children of
> Israel, and I will bless them.[9]

God blesses us with His covenants as He promises to care for us. His Word is His written contract, written first on tablets of stone then inscribed on our hearts.[10]

Fifth, we have His wine. (No pun intended!) Wine has always symbolized joy in Scripture. In the First Testament Passover, wine was used in remembrance of the passing over of the angel of death during the plague of the death of the firstborn.[11] The blood applied to the doorposts of God's people spared them from annihilation. Jesus celebrated the Passover in the same way and then became our Passover Lamb. He spoke of the cup of suffering that He would drink on our behalf. The blood of His sacrifice on the cross is credited to us so that we can enter into the presence of God. Because of Jesus's

---

[8] James 1:17
[9] Numbers 6:24–27
[10] 2 Corinthians 3:3
[11] Exodus 12

provision, our fellowship with the Father has been restored. We can remain united to the Father. Jesus's blood satisfied the wrath that separated us, in our sin, from a holy God. We celebrate the salvation and rescue that He provided on the cross for us when we celebrate communion. There is no one or nothing else that can accomplish this restoration for us, only our heavenly bridegroom, Who bought us back from the slave block of sin.

Sixth, we have His ring. Jesus stated that He had to ascend to heaven in order for the Holy Spirit to be given.[12] Ephesians says that the Holy Spirit has been given as a guarantee,[13] a pledge given in advance as a seal ensuring our home with Him forever. It is the deposit provided by our bridegroom, Jesus. The Greek word for *deposit*[14] signifies that His Spirit is our engagement ring, given to us to secure His promise of love and of His return. We are set apart for Him, and He will return for us. His covenant with us is everlasting into eternity.[15]

Seventh, He has my dowry. When I make a commitment to Christ to be His, I present my dowry. I hand over all that I have and all that I am to Him. My entire life is set aside for Him to use as He sees fit. When I agree to His covenant, I become set apart for Him alone. That is when I become "perfected." This is how Scripture states it: "For by one offering He has perfected forever those who are being sanctified."[16]

Jesus's offering is perfect in the Father's sight and the Father sees me through Jesus. Nothing more is needed. I am perfected in Him, but following His perfection is my sanctification. That is the ongoing process of renewing my mind and conforming me to the image of Jesus.[17] These are the days, in Gomer's life, where she stumbles and strays, doubts, and runs away. But symbolizing our ever-pursuing God, Hosea continues to buy her back, rescue her from the arms of

---

[12] John 16:7
[13] Ephesians 1:13–14
[14] Strong's Concordance #728, ARRABON
[15] Jeremiah 32:40
[16] Hebrews 10:14
[17] Romans 8:29

cheap love, and bring her back to himself. So even when I give Him my life to use as He sees fit then snatch it back, even when I give Him my future then crane my neck around the corner to see what's ahead, He continues to honor my heart's desire to be His. I am His perfected work in progress!

Eighth, He is the only One who can annul our covenant. He has promised that nothing will deter Him from His pursuit of me. I may have run out long ago when the going got tough, but I would have perished in the run. He knows that I need Him, and He will not let me go. The heavenly bridegroom will never serve me a certificate of divorce or leave me a widow for that matter! Therein lies the good news!

Ninth, the wedding canopy speaks of the shelter of His wings under which we take refuge.[18] As the bride and groom stand together under the canopy, we can stand with our heavenly bride-groom together before the Father, safely kept. And any marriage that is united in Christ is a three-fold cord not easily broken.[19] If we allow Him, He will bind us to Himself for eternity as a couple and as His very own. But I must stay in the canopy in the shelter of His wings. He will not hold me as prisoner there, but He promises my safety and security as I choose to abide there with Him.

Tenth, from the time we say "yes" to Jesus we are in a time of preparation. There is this waiting period that we all must endure. We are wanting to be together with Him and to be free from the cares of the day, but we are not yet ready.

I am expected to prepare for Him. While waiting, the bride prepares her wedding gown of fine linen. In Scripture, the bride is generously provided with the fine linen she needs to wear.

"Let us be glad and rejoice and give Him glory, for the marriage of the Lamb has come, and His wife has made herself ready." And to her it was granted to be arrayed in fine linen, clean and bright, for the fine linen is the righteous acts of the saints.[20]

---

[18] Psalm 91:4
[19] Ecclesiastes 4:12
[20] Revelation 19:7–8

We are clothed in Christ.[21] He has provided us with the fine linen we need to wear. It is His blood that covers us and makes us righteous before the Father. Our own righteous acts are like filthy rags[22] before Him. His is the only fine linen that will properly cover us.

I never felt more beautiful on earth than the day I was dressed in my wedding gown, prepared for my groom. It was not elaborate or expensive, but it was specifically made for that day. It was made by my mother, so there was many, many fittings and alterations. But in the end, it was worth it. I was, in my own eyes, radiant from the inside out. I was being joined to the love of my life forever. Nothing could make me happier. Until death do us part was not even a consideration at that point. Jesus is the one who makes us radiant, and nothing can separate us from His love.[23] Ernie may have been separated from our union, but he is not lost. I know where he is, and I long for the day we will be reunited together with Jesus.

In looking back in my mind's eye, I see the church where we were married. I see us standing at the altar together, and I see the cross that was suspended over us as we made our promises before God and our friends and family to each other. Today, I hear my Savior say, "*This* is how much I love you. I am uniting you with this man to display to you what love is and to teach you how to walk in it." It was not always easy. Transformation and conformation never are.

Have you ever witnessed a butterfly emerging from its chrysalis? It is brutal to watch, and it takes much restraint to not try to help it emerge. Perhaps that's just the recovering control freak in me. But if the process is "helped," the result is a butterfly that is handicapped at least and unable to survive at worst. When God tells us that He will work all things together for good, it means He will do whatever it takes to conform us to the image of His Son.[24] Some days, our marriage was hearts and flowers. Other days, it was iron sharpening

---

[21] Galatians 3:27 NIV
[22] Isaiah 64:6
[23] Romans 8:39
[24] Romans 8:28–29

iron.[25] But all days were toward a purpose. The loss of Ernie was devastating and life-changing for me. My life, as I knew it, was over. But all of it is working together, even now, to conform me into the bride that God desires. For that, I am grateful.

Eleventh, in my preparation, I cannot grow weary.[26] I must remember the bridal price Jesus paid for me. He paid the highest price of His life. The cross reminds me that He loves me enough to die for me and that He promised to come back for me. I must be expectantly awaiting His return. No one knows the day or the hour,[27] so I must always be ready to hear the shofar and see Him approaching for me. The wedding will take place in the Father's perfect time, not mine.

Twelfth, Jesus is preparing for my arrival. He promised that He is preparing a place for me in the Father's house.[28] There is no question that it is a far better place than the place I am right now. I have been blessed beyond measure on this earth, but nothing can compare to what awaits me in heaven. I am just passing through here. I am a citizen of heaven,[29] and my assignment is to take as many others home with me as I can when I leave. There is going to be a party complete with wine, food, and celebration. There will be unspeakable joy to be reunited with the love of my earthly life as we stand together and worship the One who joined us together for His glory! Now *that's* a party!

But for now, I wait. He promised that He would return for me to bring me home.[30] In the meantime, time can be mean. We need comfort, and He has provided that too. He promised that He would not leave us orphans,[31] but the Father would send the Spirit to be *in* us, even closer than Jesus was to people when He walked the earth. Though I can't see Him, He is as close as I will allow Him to be.

---

[25] Proverbs 27:17
[26] Galatians 6:9
[27] Matthew 24:36
[28] John 14:3
[29] Philippians 3:20
[30] John 14:3
[31] John 14:16–18

If you have known a beautiful love on earth, you have had a small glimpse of what God intends for us. If you have lost that love, we have the hope that we will be reunited with our earthly love[32] and will worship our heavenly bridegroom, the Giver of all good things, together again. If you have never known that kind of love, hold on. It's coming. He promised. Even death cannot separate us. Stay close, wait expectantly, be ready. He will return in His perfect time, and we will know a joy that is unspeakable.[33]

Lord, thank You for Your covenant with me. Thank You that You are the perfect bridegroom. You have stated Your intent and paid the highest of bridal prices to secure my place with You forever. You will never break Your covenant with me. Thank You that, even when I stray and am lured away by the deception of false lovers, You continually pursue me. Thank You that Your provisions are perfect as is Your timing. Thank You for Your Word that continually reminds me of Your perfect love for me and Your relentless pursuit. Our future is for eternity.

"For I am jealous for you with godly jealousy. For I have betrothed you to one husband, that I may present you as a chaste virgin to Christ" (2 Corinthians 11:2).

---

[32] 1 Thessalonians 4:17
[33] 1 Peter 1:8

PART 3

Treasures of Darkness

I will give you the treasures of darkness and hidden riches
of secret places, That you may know that I, the LORD,
Who calls you by your name, Am the God of Israel.
—Isaiah 45:3

CHAPTER 11

The Ephod

The concept of "treasures of darkness" seems almost like an oxymoron. What treasures could possibly be found in the darkness? Isn't the darkness something to be avoided? Weren't we always told to be home before the streetlights go on to avoid being out in the darkness? Don't only frightening things happen in the darkness?

The apostle John had one of the most intimate relationships with our Lord Jesus Christ recorded in Scripture. He is repeatedly referred to as the disciple whom Jesus loved.[1] After Jesus washed His disciples' feet, He foretold of His soon coming betrayal. John's position during this discussion is described as "leaning on Jesus' bosom."[2] "John knew the heartbeat of Jesus and he explicitly tells us "God is light; in Him there is no darkness at all."[3]

So what do we do when we find ourselves in the darkness? What do we do when we find ourselves lost in an unfamiliar place with no light to guide us, with no idea where we are going? What do we do when we are frightened of what lurks in that darkness, and we fear what might be ahead?

One option is to curl up into the fetal position and hide, hoping that the monsters there will not see us as we wait for the darkness to

---

[1] John 13:23, 19:26, 21:7, 21:20
[2] John 13:23
[3] 1 John 1:5

pass, if it ever will. Another option is to run randomly trying to find a way out, hitting wall after wall until we collapse with exhaustion. A third option is to hear the words of Isaiah and search for the treasures and riches hidden there. It is to seek out God for Who He really is and to hear Him calling our name.

We may have to do some serious mining to unearth them, but God the Father promises that there are treasures and riches hidden in the darkness. These are not treasures of monetary value. They will not bring us fame and fortune in this world. These are treasures of eternal value. These treasures will cause us to know Him better. They will bring us wealth and fortune that the world knows nothing about.

The treasures are free for the taking if we humble ourselves and admit that we cannot find our way out on our own. As we admit that we are helpless to rescue ourselves and ask for a Savior, Jesus is faithful and compassionate to come alongside us and even take up residence with us and travel to the other side of the darkness.

God never promised us that we would never see darkness. Rather, Jesus promised, "In this world you *will* have trouble. But take heart! I have overcome the world"[4] (emphasis added). So let's unearth some treasures. Let's move some dirt and plow away some worldly attitudes and preconceptions. This is a process that Scripture describes as being "transformed by the renewing of your mind."[5]

Treasures and riches are waiting. God promises that we will know Him better as we unearth those treasures. *That's* eternal life right here on planet Earth! Jesus tells us, "Now this is eternal life: that they may know You, the only true God, and Jesus Christ, Whom You have sent."[6]

David found himself in deep darkness. This is the same David who, as a young boy, was minding his own business tending the sheep. Though overlooked at first as the youngest and the least likely candidate, he ends up being anointed by God by the prophet Samuel

---

[4] John 16:33
[5] Romans 12:2
[6] John 17:3

as king over Israel, God's people.[7] What an honor and responsibility for young David. I wonder what David's initial perception was of his honored anointing. Did he imagine himself reclining on his throne in the palace being entertained by the court jester? Did he, in his mind, taste the choicest food prepared by the best chefs in Israel? Did he see himself surrounded by gold and riches, never wanting for anything?

David was so much more spiritual that I am. I'm sure he didn't wrestle with that spirit of entitlement, thinking that he deserved comfort and ease. I, on the other hand, have my own throne. As I sit with my feet up in my recliner, entertained by my own court jester, the television, I contemplate why I must face times of trial and darkness. After all, I am royalty by means of the blood of my Savior Jesus. He has bought for me a place in the King's family, a room in the Father's house. But I am not "home" yet.

As I wait for the time to enter my own mansion prepared for me by King Jesus in my Father's house,[8] I must, like David, wait for God's perfect timing. While David waited, he faced many times of deep darkness and confusion. The first thing that most people remember about David is his battle with Goliath.[9] As a young boy, untrained in battle maneuvers, without armor or fear, David stood before the giant "in the name of the Lord Almighty."[10] The name David used, in the original language is "YHWH."[11] This is the tetragrammaton, the proper and covenant name of God. It describes God's personal relationship with his people. The Jews never spoke this name for fear of offending a holy God. This was Almighty God's unspeakable Name. It was not spoken aloud as it portrayed an aspect of God too great to be adequately described by mere words. It was a concept too great to be conveyed verbally but could only be known or perceived internally. To try to express it in language would only

---

[7] 1 Samuel 16:13
[8] John 14:2
[9] 1 Samuel 17
[10] 1 Samuel 17:45
[11] Strong's concordance #3068, YHVH

diminish or weaken its real meaning. We know this name as Yahweh or Jehovah.

David knew His God even as a young boy. He spent many hours in quiet meditation while tending his father's sheep. He had experienced God's protection repeatedly. This was his training ground for the assignment God had planned for him. He learned to listen carefully for the voice of God. When the time came to put into practice what he had learned about God, there was no hesitation, no doubt, and no fear. He stood firmly in the name of the Lord God Almighty. He knew he was not standing alone before the giant, Goliath. He knew that the battle was his Lord's. David was not afraid of Goliath because he knew the bigness of his God. David was the vessel through whom God would be victorious. "The LORD who delivered me from the paw of the lion and the paw of the bear will deliver me from the hand of this Philistine."[12]

With his confidence in His God, David stood before Goliath with five smooth stones and a sling. One shot was all it took for the giant to be felled. As the defeated giant lay on the ground, David ran up to grab Goliath's sword to cut off his head. David knew that it was "not by the sword or the spear"[13] that the giant was defeated but by the Lord God Almighty. Immediately, King Saul took David into his service at the palace. David succeeded in everything he did and gained the trust and respect of the people.

Saul became jealous of David's popularity and turned against him. Repeatedly, Saul tried to kill David. Eventually, David, running in fear for his life, ended up in Nob, begging for help from the resident priest. Interestingly enough, he was searching for a sword or spear to help protect him. The priest replied, "The sword of Goliath the Philistine, whom you killed in the Valley of Elah, is here; it is wrapped in a cloth *behind the ephod*. If you want it, take it; there is no sword here but that one" (emphasis added). David said, "There is none like it; give it to me."[14]

---

[12] 1 Samuel 17:37

[13] 1 Samuel 17:47

[14] 1 Samuel 21:9

When I first studied that portion of Scripture, I felt compelled to consider the phrase "behind the ephod." The Holy Spirit seemed to illuminate that phrase for me so that I needed to investigate it more. It seemed that the ephod was not just an incidental finding covering the defeated sword. God was saying, "Don't miss the ephod."

What is an ephod? God gave very specific instructions for the tabernacle that the Israelites were to build in the wilderness. These instructions included details regarding the priestly garments. The ephod was one of the pieces included in the priestly attire. It attached to the breastplate and bore two onyx stones mounted in gold filigree on each shoulder. The individual names of the tribes of Israel were "engraved like a signet or seal on each onyx stone as a memorial before the Lord."[15] Why would this be significant to David? The onyx stones were engraved with the individual names of those God loved, His chosen people. The prophet Isaiah spoke on behalf of God regarding engraving as well.

"Can a mother forget the baby at her breast and have no compassion on the child she has borne? Though she may forget, I will not forget you! See, I have engraved you on the palms of my hands; your walls are ever before me."[16]

Our names are recorded and permanently etched on the palms of God's hand. That's how much He cares for us. He can never forget us or let us wander off His radar screen. He loves us far too much. We are sealed for Him, today, by His Holy Spirit,[17] as His own possession for eternity when we receive Jesus.

The darkness had closed in on David and had obscured his memory and his vision. In the darkness, David forgot how God had protected him and fought his battles for him in the field with his sheep as well as on the battlefront with Goliath. David forgot what he had said over the slain body of Goliath, "the LORD does not save with sword and spear; for the battle *is* the LORD's."[18] David forgot that he belonged to God and that God would continue to protect

---

[15] Exodus 39:6
[16] Isaiah 49:15–16
[17] Ephesians 1:13–14
[18] 1 Samuel 17:47

him in each and every situation. David belonged to God. His name was engraved like a seal on the palm of God's hand in the same way that the twelve tribes of Israel were engraved on the ephod.

At Nob, David was offered two weapons: the defeated sword of Goliath or the ephod. What protection could the ephod offer? It was a memorial of God's constant and perfect protection when we cannot protect ourselves. God had always fought on David's behalf but this time, David chose the defeated sword. Without calling on his heritage in God, He continued running for his life. He had been anointed as king. This was probably not the life of royalty he had envisioned. David's first experience in leading people rather than sheep began as he hid from Saul in the cave of Adullum. Here is where David's Three-D ministry was born. "All those in distress or in debt or discontented gathered around him, and he became their leader. About four hundred men were with him."[19] A challenging ministry for even the best of leaders!

No matter where David turned at this point, whether back to the sheep pasture or staying holed up in the cave, he was surrounded by a whole lot of bleating! David missed his treasure in the darkness but not forever. The good news is that God still used him mightily to accomplish His purpose. He became a powerful and God-fearing king who continued to make mistakes. His mistakes were never fatal, as they never are in God. He is still considered a "man after God's own heart."[20] The ephod of God's promise endured.

For me this, means that the next time I am faced with a fight-or-flight response, I must remember God's past faithfulness. I must remember His present promises and His secure plans for the future. I pray that I not grab a defeated strategy but that I will see His provision right in front of me. I pray to hear His voice over the fear and panic and listen for His direction. The first choice that God offers is probably His perfect option. If I miss Him the first time, He will

---

[19] 1 Samuel 22:2
[20] 1 Samuel 13:14

continue to keep me in a place where the bleating is likely to drive me back to Him. His greatest desire is that I know Him more and more.

Lord, thank You that You have engraved me on the palm of Your Hand. Thank You that You are always there in fear and battle to offer Your strength over my own strategy. Help me to pause and see it. Help me not to blow past Your perfect provision for me and reach for a defeated weapon in my own strength. I am Yours. You know my name. You will protect me in all things for the glory of Your Name. Thank You, Lord, for treasures in darkness.

> "No weapon formed against you shall prosper,
> And every tongue which rises against you in
> judgment
> You shall condemn.
> This is the heritage of the servants of the LORD,
> And their righteousness is from Me,"
> Says the LORD. (Isaiah 54:17)

CHAPTER 12

The Gym

Have you ever been given a gift intended to increase your strength and endurance? Perhaps a gym membership? Maybe it was a gift from someone, or it was a gift to yourself. You are aware, at the onset, that you are weaker than you want to be. Your endurance is not enough to carry you and you are out of shape. You know your weakness and your goal is to get stronger and more fit. You resign yourself to the fact that it's going to take time and work. You realize that it's not going to be fun all the time. You may meet new people along the way who encourage you in your fitness journey. You may even have a coach or a personal trainer who will not let you quit. You may build new friendships that extend outside of the gym. You meet some people who are very skilled in this pursuit of fitness, and you meet some who are dragging themselves into the gym every day as beginners, like yourself.

If we are going to be fit for the kingdom of God, we need to pursue spiritual training as well. Scripture describes it this way: "Now no chastening seems to be joyful for the present, but painful; nevertheless, afterward it yields the peaceable fruit of righteousness to those who have been trained by it."[1]

The word *chastening* in the Greek is specific to training up a child. It means giving instructions that train someone to reach full develop-

---

[1]   Hebrews 12:11

ment and maturity.[2] It is something that will cause pain, as weak muscles are worked to increase their strength. We also know it can be painful to discipline a child. But to allow them to continue in disobedience will only lead to destruction. Discipline is an act of love that is painful to both the parent and the child but strengthens them both in correct behavior. It gives the child the skills necessary to manage their life and overcome the struggles that will come their way. To ignore discipline produces a child who lacks endurance and survival skills. We cannot avoid the pain of strengthening spiritual muscles any more that we can avoid the pain of discipline and strengthening physical muscles.

The yield or the result of discipline is peace. It promises an ability to endure, without distress, the weight of whatever we are asked to lift. It is not the removal of challenges, but it is having confidence to know that we are not unprepared. We are certain that we have built up the strength we need to endure. That peace, according to Scripture, is in regard to righteousness. That is, to be able to act in ways that are God-approved. We can become "useful for the Master, prepared for every good work,"[3] confident that we have been trained up in the way that will please God, provide our peace and bring Him glory.

For me, the key word in that Scripture is "trained." We can endure discipline but not be trained by it. We can gain experience but not wisdom. We can walk away from the chastening unchanged and have to start over from square one when we are faced with the same challenge. Wisdom is the practical application of what I have learned in the experience that strengthens me to do better the next time. The Greek translation of the word *trained* describes it perfectly:

Gymnázō ("exert intensely, like a pro-athlete") presumes full discipline, necessary to be in "top working condition" (full agility, skill, endurance). This is gained only from *constant*, rigorous training (exercise). *Gymnázō* conveys acquiring *proficiency through practice*—regular exercise with graduated resistance (the physical element is also included with the spiritual of being in "God's gymnasium").[4]

---

2   Strong's concordance #3809, PAIDEIA
3   2 Timothy 2:21
4   Strong's concordance #1128, GYMNAZO

There you have it. God takes His children to His gym to train them in His way of survival and peace because He loves us and knows what will build us up, not destroy us. He knows how to change us for the best because He knows what's ahead.

This was my experience in 1993. Ernie and I had four daughters, aged sixteen, fourteen, twelve, and two. We had settled in after finally being able to adopt Jenna into our family after eighteen months of some uncertainty. Construction of an in-law apartment in our house was complete to provide for my father, who was in increasing need of assistance. For my father to become part of our household was the culmination of a long road to reconciliation. He had struggled in many areas for most of his life, which affected our relationship, as well as many areas of my life. But now, forgiveness had given way to the ability to provide a safer place for him as well as provide him with the help he needed.

Things seemed to be working to everyone's benefit for eight months. The children were getting to know him better, he seemed to be enjoying them, and it seemed that most of his needs were being met. Then one morning in August, I discovered that he had committed a violent suicide in his apartment. There was no warning, no reason that was made known to us, no signs that we could recall. For us, it was out of the blue. Our world collapsed in one devastating moment. I was shocked, terrified, confused, saddened, angry, and sworn to secrecy as to the cause of his death. Secrecy was the way I had been "trained." My learned way of survival was to present a "white-picket fence" existence in the face of chaos. This was how I had lived my life up to this point.

Needless to say, we had a lot to work through in our immediate and extended family as we moved forward. But move forward we did. We had the apartment cleaned, and we closed it up for many months as if it didn't exist. We limped along, and I was continually consumed with a cloud of fear and confusion that would not let up. As hard as I tried to press through, I had too much inside me that I was terrified to let out. I became unable to work effectively and I lost interest in outside activities. I was barely able to take care of myself and my family. Joy was lost under a smoldering heap of suppressed emotions. I failed counselling a few times. It took many years for me to realize that the only common denominator in that failed counselling equation was *me*! I had built a double-ditch, walled-in refuge for myself that kept others out and kept me imprisoned. This is where God brought me to His gym.

A couple of months later, we learned that Jenna's birth mother was expecting another baby. Because we had adopted Jenna into our family, child protective services asked us if we would consider taking this child into foster care and, once again, try to teach parenting. Our house was full of girls, so if the baby was a boy, that would not be an option. I secretly prayed that it would be a boy. I was unable to care for myself or the family I had. How would I ever be able to take care of another baby, especially if it was as fragile as Jenna was when she came home? How would I be able to extend myself even further to try to teach parenting again to this birth mother? I said that I "prayed" that it was a boy, but that is not really accurate. In my turmoil, the faith that I had known had crumbled in the aforementioned smoldering heap of suppressed emotions.

The day came when the baby was born. My NICU nurse practitioner friend called me at home. He said, "It's a girl." God said, "Okay, Rickson, suit up. We're going to the gym." Caitlin was born only three weeks before her due date, but she weighed only three and a half pounds. She had "tried" to be born at twenty-nine weeks gestation, eleven weeks prematurely, but the doctors were able to stop labor. Jenna had been born at twenty-nine weeks, weighing in at two and a half pounds. She, however, grew to more normal newborn size and development in an incubator until she came home at three months of age. Caitlin had not grown as well in the womb. She was very tiny but fully developed. The challenge was to overcome her small size and her failure-to-thrive. Still being drawn to babies and challenges. I was willing to engage. It didn't make any earthly sense, but then again, His ways are not our ways.[5] So here I was, a shell of a human being, taking on another human being. But God knew the plan.

---

[5] Isaiah 55:8

Bringing Caitlin home allowed me to take a family leave from the nursery. This was necessary as my empathy and patience for families who desperately needed it was severely lacking. I was so busy trying to hold myself together that there was nothing left for others in need. I was not a good nurse or even a good person at that point.

Being responsible for this fragile infant caused me to have to come out of myself and the wounded world in which I found myself hostage. I was in a prison of my own making in my own home. Caitlin was a new focus, and Ernie and the girls rose to the challenge of caring for another baby. It was a joyful new diversion for all of us. She was a new little life that needed our love and attention.

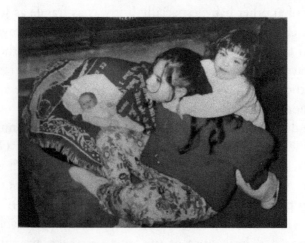

Because I had allowed my faith to crumble, the hunger I had experienced for God's Word since the day I committed my life to Him had, quite frankly, turned to repulsion. I no longer continued my daily habit of Bible reading. I was starving myself to death because I could not fathom why God had allowed this violent act to harm us. I was used to my father's harm, but I vowed that it would never touch my family. I continued to be angry and confused. But that did not deter my loving, persistent God. Though I did not crack my Bible, I had been given a calendar that contained a daily Scripture. It sat next to the rocking chair I used to feed Caitlin every three hours, day and night. I was unable to consume any quantity of Scripture at that moment, but this small, repeated dose of Scripture was the perfect prescribed amount to open up my eyes and my heart once again. It took many months to begin to break free, but it also took many months of feeding this fragile infant a perfectly prescribed amount of formula, repeatedly, so she could grow, an ounce at a time. We were growing and healing together.

And grow she did. We no longer had to be concerned about her falling through the couch cushions because she was so small! She, however, began to miss meeting developmental milestones that caused concern. To understand how God preserves babies in the womb is to understand His unrelenting love for us. You see, even in a hostile environment, where the baby is not able to take in the nutrients needed to grow, the baby's brain is guarded. Other parts of the baby will be compromised so that the brain can be fed. That is why Caitlin was so small at birth. Her body was malnourished. But unfortunately, the environment was so hostile that even her brain ended up being compromised. If a baby is born only small for dates, they will be tiny but still have a normal head size. They will continue to grow after birth and eventually catch up with their peers in all areas. If, however, the baby's brain had suffered insult, the head size will be smaller than normal, confirming the brain injury. They will be small physically and also be compromised neurologically. After birth, they will continue to grow physically but be delayed developmentally. That was the case with Caitlin. Not only was her body small, but her head size was smaller than expected at birth. Though, she continued to grow in size, she was delayed in development. In the end, Caitlin's birth mother was not able to consistently care for her. After another eighteen months of uncertainty, Cait became another chosen member of our family.

To this day, thirty years later, Caitlin continues to be challenged in many areas of her life. Her behavior and emotional responses have always been her most difficult challenge. She historically would default to aggression or self-injurious behavior in response to any stress. She can still be vulnerable to overstimulation and respond in destructive ways. I have often thought that some days caring for her would kill me, but she was sent to save my life. At a time that I had nothing left, God knew exactly what I needed to come out of myself. He knew that this fragile infant would cut through my consuming grief and confusion. He knew exactly the "training" I needed. It was not to kill me. It was to strengthen me and give me endurance for what He knew I would need for what was ahead. He especially strengthened the faith that I would desperately need for the future. In my bruised and smoldering state. God proved His Word: "A bruised reed He will not break, And smoking flax He will not quench" (Matthew 12:20).

There is a story told by Dan Winkler in his book *Forgiven, Forgiving and Free*. He tells of a four-year old who was praying according to Matthew 6:14–15. What this little boy repeated was profound. "Lord, forgive us our trash baskets as we forgive those who put trash in our baskets." I had to clear out a lot of trash while moving forward but God was faithful and careful to bring me step by step in line with His plan. He continues to clear out my trash basket every day as I come to Him and give Him access.

Caitlin has grown to be a very spiritually sensitive young woman. She has given me insight into things that I would have missed if she was not "mine." I have met absolutely amazing people because of her. These are people skilled in special needs who have shown us the way. There have been many heroes who have come into Caitlin's and our family's life, and it has been an honor and a privilege to get to know each of them. They have been vital to our survival. Unfortunately, I have also offended some people in my attempts to make the right choice. I have needed to learn to forgive those who choose not to forgive me. I have needed to learn to "entrust myself to the One Who judges justly."[6] Circling back to the trash comparison, in my home, I need to dispose of my trash at a place called the transfer station. I transfer the things I don't need and that stink up my life to this place made to handle it. Spiritually, I also need to transfer the things that weigh me down and stink up my life to God, Who knows how to properly deal with them.

---

[6] 1 Peter 2:23

Through the darkness of my gym experience, I have found treasures that many who don't have children with special needs overlook. It is not the journey I was expecting but I can truly say I continue to be trained by it.

A body builder doesn't ask the trainer to remove the weight but seeks strength to be able to lift it. Jesus Himself prayed, "Not My will but Yours,"[7] then He was strengthened. His goal for me is not comfort and leisure but to be conformed into the strength and endurance of His Son.[8] He is building me into His princess warrior to follow Him resolutely through the trials and temptations that come my way in ways that please Him. He exposes my weaknesses and then provides His strength to overcome them. I am grateful that my loving coach didn't allow me to quit even at my lowest. I am grateful that He was not turned away by my rejection in my confusion. Instead, He gave me room to see His light, one glimmer at a time. He has graciously shown me what adoption means in the good and the challenging. He has adopted me into His family,[9] for better or for worse.

Some days I would have sold this journey to the lowest bidder, but today, I have been changed. I see that the strength and faith He has built in me has allowed me to endure other hard things and to encourage others. I consider this journey a priceless treasure even as it was wrapped in thick darkness!

Lord, thank You for taking me to Your gym. Thank You that You took me at my weakest and built me up from there. I am grateful that You loved me enough to not leave me undisciplined. You proved Your promise to turn my ash heap into beauty for Your glory alone. Thank You that you used a helpless infant to bring me back to You. Just as You placed yourself in the form of a Baby in a manger, You used my least likely expectation to show me Who You are. You have given me a family that I so desired and You adopted me into Your

---

[7] Luke 22:42
[8] Romans 8:29
[9] Ephesians 1:5

eternal family. For that. I am grateful. My desire is to surrender more and more to You so You can make me fit for Your use.

> To console those who mourn in Zion,
> To give them beauty for ashes,
> The oil of joy for mourning,
> The garment of praise for the spirit of heaviness;
> That they may be called trees of righteousness,
> The planting of the LORD, that He may be glori-
> fied. (Isaiah 61:3)

CHAPTER 13

Advanced Training

My training did not end with my gym experience with Caitlin. Thirteen years later, my beloved Ernie would leave the home he had prepared for us and go on to the home prepared for him by His Savior in heaven. I became a widow and a single parent to five children—one married, two in college, and two still at home. You can read about my initial steps in the darkness of widowhood and the treasures hidden there in my book *A Walk Through the Shadow*.

I still had a part time staff nurse position in the NICU to support myself financially. It had been thirty years of caring for preemies. I know that somewhere along the line I had grand-preemies and perhaps even great-grand preemies. It had also been thirty years of working every other weekend and holiday. Now that Ernie was gone, I was struggling with the thought of leaving my children to go to work on the upcoming holidays. Even though Jenna had outgrown the need for a babysitter at thirteen, she still needed someone to watch over her decisions on weekends. And Caitlin required trained care when I was away and that could be undependable. Yes, the stretching was audible.

Ernie had always wanted me to consider a job that wasn't so stressful and demanding, possibly an outpatient position that didn't require working weekends and holidays. Unknown to me, before he left, he had been working on this behind the scenes. At one point in his cancer treatment, he needed a blood transfusion, which was given at our local hospital where I worked. He was cared for by two of my former NICU colleagues, Betsy and Holly. They were piloting an outpatient pediatric procedure unit called the Comfort Zone. While I was out for coffee during his transfusion, Ernie talked to them about ways to get me out of NICU into an outpatient job. There were openings to be posted in the Comfort Zone and Ernie suggested that I apply. I shrugged off his suggestion knowing that I didn't have the energy to learn a whole new set of skills. At this point, I knew preemies and preemies was all I knew and all I would ever know. Hmmmm. There is a hint of Lot's wife there, isn't there? Stuck in the past and blind to the future.

After Ernie died, I needed to reconsider his suggestion. Not only were the weekends and holidays difficult but being at work for 7:00 a.m. required that someone else get Caitlin on the school bus. This task was, at times, very challenging. She would often resist to the point where it would take a trained person from the Howard Center crisis team to make it happen. And even if she got to school, she would resist going in the building. The school would then call me to come and bring her home. Managing Caitlin in a public school was an incredible challenge and a steep learning curve for all of us. There were, however, no other options. Trust me. I searched for them all.

Caitlin's developmental and behavioral challenges were difficult enough without being exacerbated by our profound grief of losing Ernie. Whatever coping skills we had left were stretched to the limit. It is here, in retrospect (looking back to see His faithfulness and certainly *not* longing to go back) that I see with undeniable certainty the power of the grace of my God. I have absolutely no idea how I survived this season in my life. These are the times when you know that you know Who God is and no one can take that from you. This was one of them!

In the meantime, while time was being mean, Betsy and Holly were faithful to keep their eyes open for any potential outpatient job openings. At one point, they suggested that I work per diem with them so that when a position became available, I would already be trained. That seemed like a reasonable risk. I still had my NICU position if I couldn't cut it. I had nothing to lose and only hope to gain. I gave it a try.

I quickly discovered that I *could* learn new skills. In fact, they were the same skills I already had but on much bigger pediatric patients. I was really enjoying doing something different. A position was posted in the Comfort Zone, and I applied and interviewed for it. This was very exciting. The hours would be very flexible so that I could get Cait on the bus every day and, of course, no weekends or holidays. How perfect! God had provided super abundantly and the timing was ideal. School would start again in a month. I could give my notice in the NICU and be well on my way. Expectations!

After my interview with the Comfort Zone manager, she said she would get back to me by the end of the week. She sounded very favorable, especially since I was already familiar with the job. I was all ready to empty my NICU locker. I waited. The end of the week came, and then the middle of the next week came. I called the manager and had to leave a message. I asked Betsy and Holly if they had heard anything. I emailed the manager. Nothing came in response to any of my communication attempts. Wait. What?

God, are You still there? It has been a very dark arduous journey getting on without Ernie. God, do You know that I'm still here? Do You know how hard it has been. Do You know all the responsibilities I have now, by myself? Do You know that school is going to start? Do You know that Thanksgiving and Christmas are coming. Do You know what Jenna is doing on weekends when I'm not here? Do You know? Do You care? Deep darkness set in again.

Playing a part in my decision to leave the NICU was also the fact that I had received a poor performance evaluation. I had always taken my responsibilities very seriously, and it was important to me to do a good job, as unto the Lord.[1] Yes, I had just come through three years of being with my husband through intensive cancer treatments. Yes, he had recently died. Yes, I was doing my very best to keep my head above water. No, my poor evaluation was not related to patient care but to committee work and continuing education. Nonetheless,

[1] Colossians 3:23

I was not making the grade. A cloud of shame descended as I saw myself unable to meet the expectations of my peers or my God. This was the straw that broke my back. It was time to move on, to get a fresh start. When people say that God never gives you more than you can handle, they are wrong. God will allow enough so that you will come to the realization that He is your only hope until you cry out for His help. He is ready and waiting with great anticipation to come to our rescue.

I never did hear from the Comfort Zone manager, but I did take a step of faith and apply for two other outpatient jobs. One was in an outlying doctor's office close to my home. The work was mostly phone triage with little physical patient contact. I decided that it was not for me. I liked to have my hands in the trenches, so to speak. But it was nice to have options.

The other job for which I applied was in a pediatric outpatient clinic at the hospital. I really had no idea what the job involved; but the hours were flexible, there was no weekends or holidays, it involved hands on pediatric care, and family education. I knew a lot of that, and I had also recently learned that I could learn new things! In addition, I was familiar with the providers who ran the clinic. The interview went very well but the nurse manager was on vacation so I would have to wait for her return before a final decision was made. I was, however getting better and better at waiting. Not good, mind you, just better.

Thankfully, I was offered the job in pediatric outpatient if I wanted it. (Are you kidding?!) I gave my notice in the NICU and started my new schedule on the first day of school for Jenna and Caitlin. I was able to get them off to school before heading off to my new assignment. I also got a pay raise so that my salary was comparable to what I left in the NICU after thirty years.

Did God know? Did God care?

For My thoughts are not your thoughts,
neither are your ways my ways, declares the Lord.

As the heavens are higher than the earth,
so are My ways higher than your ways and My
thoughts than your thoughts.[2]

I had originally seen my poor performance evaluation as another setback. It was the first time I had ever been "reprimanded" for my work. In retrospect, again, I see that it was not a setback but a setup, a stepping stone to the place God was leading me. All the while He was leading me, I was bleating and complaining that my dark and arduous journey was too hard. I was blinded to His presence and His faithfulness.

This experience reminds me of the account of Martha and Mary.[3] Martha is busy preparing a meal for which Jesus never asked. She is frustrated by Jesus's seemingly lack of concern for her self-imposed load of work. She asked Jesus if He cared. In essence, she was saying. "Don't You see what needs to happen here?" In response, Jesus lovingly calls her by name, not once but twice. "Martha, Martha." He confirmed that He knew her frustration, but He had a better way. It was like He was saying to her, "Don't *you* see what needs to happen here?" Jesus invited Martha to sit at His feet, to take His yoke upon her and learn from Him.[4] *That* was the place where she would find rest and the proper motivation to serve that would not drain her of all her resources. Jesus did not shame Martha but gently led her out of her prison of performance and perfection to find His strength.

After this, Martha had another training with Jesus. This time, it was at the grave of her brother Lazarus.[5] Martha had called for Jesus when Lazarus became ill, but Jesus intentionally delayed His departure. By the time Jesus arrived, Lazarus had been dead for four days. Jewish belief was that the spirit of a person hovered for three days after death and then departed. By this time, Lazarus was not only dead. He was really, really dead without hope and the whole thing stunk!

---

[2]   Isaiah 55:8–9
[3]   Luke 10:38–42
[4]   Matthew 11:29
[5]   John 11:1–44

When Jesus finally arrived, Martha ran to Him. She stated her confidence that if Jesus had been there, Lazarus would not have died. It sounds much like an accusation, but she followed it up with her hope of Jesus's favor with God to do something. It was like Martha was saying, "Lord, You knew what needed to happen here, but now it's too late." It doesn't seem like she expected a resurrection because when Jesus commanded that the grave be opened, Martha warned Jesus of the impending stench of death. But Jesus was growing her faith. He was saying to her, "Martha, *this* is what needs to happen here!" He wanted her to see and experience the glory of God like she never had before. Martha had confessed her belief in what she already knew about Jesus,[6] but she was uncertain that there was more. Jesus was certain that there *was* more. He wanted to reveal Himself as the Resurrection and the Life,[7] as the victor over death and the grave. Martha's expectations were exceeded. (Unlike the expectations on my performance evaluation but that, too, was used to squeeze me into the place He desired for me.)

When my expectations are upended, I still have a tendency to freak out. It takes a deliberate decision to chillax and come to Jesus with confidence and not condemnation. Instead of "Don't You care?" I can affirm, "I *know* You care!" Then I can ask Him to show me the treasure He wants me to see and find rest in Him as He promised.

Jesus did come as an infant, as promised. He did walk among us and experience the full range of human emotions and more. He did conquer death, hell, and the grave as the perfect Lamb of God, as He promised. I can't fully understand it all. My three-pound brain cannot contain an infinite God. But I can trust Him because He has shown Himself trustworthy time and time and time again on my behalf.

He came as Prince of Peace[8] to dwell with us and in us as Immanuel.[9] We are not alone. The increase of His government will

---

[6] John 11:27
[7] John 11:25
[8] Isaiah 9:6
[9] Isaiah 7:14

have no end.[10] The promise has not reached it final fulfillment, but it will. He is coming back for us to bring us home if we are willing to receive Him.[11] And He will reign as Victor over the final battle in the end. I don't know when or precisely how it will all happen, but I am expectantly unexpectant, trusting Him. He has never given me a reason for mistrust.

Lord, thank You that You have never left me alone. Thank You for experiences that prove Your endless faithfulness. Thank You that you call me by name and are patient with my humanity because You have personally experienced it. Continue to reveal Yourself to me in deeper and more meaningful ways in whatever way You desire. Keep me close when I freak out and do what only You can do. You are trustworthy.

"For I know the thoughts that I think toward you, says the LORD, thoughts of peace and not of evil, to give you a future and a hope" (Jeremiah 29:11).

---

[10] Isaiah 9:7
[11] John 14:3

CHAPTER 14

Love

Love is something for which we all have an innate need and desire. We were created in the image of God,[1] and God is love.[2] Love is an expression of who we are. It may be the love of a parent, a spouse, or a friend but we spend our lifetime searching for it. Some of us can celebrate that we have experienced love as God intended it in a human relationship. Some of us are mourning the loss of that love by means of death, abandonment, or divorce. Some are stuck in a harmful place where they had hoped that love would be found. Some are in the continual pursuit of love and are growing weary. Some have a distorted idea of what love is and are on a search for the impossible, outside of God. Some have never found love as God intended it and have settled for cheap substitutes. Can you identify with one or more of these scenarios?

We know in our heads that God is love. He does not just give love. It is the essence of Who He is. He cannot *not* love. Sometimes His ways may not seem loving, but the truth is that *all* He does is out of love. He has no selfish, hidden agenda or motives. His love is not like human love, and often our human experiences distort the truth of His love. God's love cannot be earned by our performance or lost by our failures.

---

[1]   Genesis 1:27
[2]   1 John 4:8

Repeatedly in his Gospel, the apostle John describes himself as "the disciple whom Jesus loved."[3] He was not being conceited or exclusive. It was not that Jesus loved John more than the others. God is not partial.[4] But John fully embraced the love of God in Christ. He was completely convinced of it, and he received it without reservation. As a result, he was able to demonstrate and communicate that love. John was not perfect, but he was perfectly loved, and he wasn't afraid to say it.

In his Gospel, John provides a beautiful picture of the perfect love of God. In chapter 8, we see Jesus sitting in the temple teaching the people. His posture of sitting is important because teachers in that culture sat while they taught as a sign of their authority. As you may know, Jesus was not well received among the religious leaders of His day even though His coming as Messiah had been prophesied in their teachings for centuries. The people were gathered around Jesus listening, hungry for His wisdom. In the midst of His teaching, some religious leaders burst in, abruptly disrupting the teaching. These men, the scribes and Pharisees, were the experts in Jewish law, and they were honored religious teachers. Their love, however, was for their own fame and for the respect and admiration of their followers.

I wonder if they were offended because Jesus was taking their position as teachers. Do you suppose they were worried that Jesus knew more than they did? Were they afraid that He might outrank them in authority? Would Jesus take their place of honor and respect among the people, exposing their inadequacies? They certainly were threatened by the attention that Jesus was gathering. And they certainly had no reservations about interrupting. They carried an attitude of entitlement to the love of God because of their heritage, their knowledge, and their credentials. Unlike John, they *were* conceited and exclusive.

Not only did they interrupt, they also cast a woman in the center of the court in which Jesus was teaching. We only know her as "this woman." She is given no name, and she is identified solely by

---

[3]   John 13:23; 19:26; 20:2; 21:7, 21
[4]   Romans 2:11

her sinful act. She was thrown center stage between Jesus and the listeners, which were, likely, mostly men. She had been caught "in the very act of adultery."[5] The religious leaders' discovery leaves a lot of questions. How did these "revered" men catch her? Were they watching? Was she a setup? Who was she with? Did they allow her to get dressed before they seized her? All conjecture aside, there she was now fully exposed before men and Jesus. At the very least, she was covered in accusation, shame, and guilt. There was no denying what she had done. Thankfully, she was before a loving Judge and not the judgmental Jewish leaders with no defense. The Pharisees love was for strict adherence to the law and not for the people it was intended to protect. Jesus's love was so much more.

I wonder what the woman was seeking before she got caught. Was she looking for love in all the wrong places? Was she coerced against her will into this act? Was she tricked into this compromising position? Was she left empty and unloved at home, looking for something more to satisfy her? I think we can all admit to being guilty of a similar search at times. Perhaps not in the act of adultery but by getting involved with someone or something we later regretted. Maybe the comfort of food, the lure of power, the draw of wealth, the spotlight of fame, compromise for the sake of acceptance. All these can lead to the same shameful outcome outside of Jesus. We all have our weaknesses, and we are all prone to judge. It's our human condition apart from Christ. Max Lucado said it something like this: "We judge others for the limp in their walk, but we can't see the tack in their shoe."[6] We are all hobbling along looking for relief.

So here she is, fully exposed with no defense or even a partner in crime. The "experts" said, according to the law, she must be stoned. That was only half right. The whole truth is this: "If a man is found lying with a woman married to a husband, then *both* of them shall die..."[7] [according to Deuteronomy] the adulterer *and* the adulteress shall surely be put to death"[8] (in Leviticus).

---

5 John 8:4

6 Max Lucado, *In the Grip of Grace* (Thomas Nelson Publishing, 1996).

7 Deuteronomy 22:22

8 Leviticus 20:10

Why was she there alone? Where was the man? Was he a Pharisee that his friends were protecting? Had he run away in shame or fear of being caught, too? But she had been caught "in the very act," so he couldn't have been too far away. He, however, had escaped the shame. The Pharisees had set this trap to see how Jesus would judge.[9] Would Jesus leave Himself open to error? Silly Pharisees! The very Word to which they pointed, the law of Moses, was the very same Word that was standing right in front of them!

Jesus did not take the bait. While the Pharisees stood in judgment, Jesus stooped down.[10] He wrote on the ground, pretending He didn't hear them. Perhaps Jesus was giving the Pharisees an opportunity to reflect on their accusation and the incomplete nature of their judgment. They had let the adulterer go free and brought the adulteress to be judged. Perhaps Jesus was stooping down to take the cold, hard stares off from the woman.

He wrote on the ground. Did He write the sins of the Pharisees in the dirt? Did He write their names and *their* lovers? Did He write the ten commandments? Did He intend to remind them that they were made from the same "dirt"[11] from which the woman was made? The religious leaders continued to press Jesus for His verdict, but Jesus was making room for His grace. He stood up and said, "He who is without sin among you, let him throw a stone at her first."[12]

All those present were disqualified because of their own sin. All except Jesus. The only One qualified to throw the first stone, stooped down again. He said nothing more and allowed their own conscience to speak to them. One by one, from the oldest and wisest and perhaps the one who had accumulated the most sin, they went away. Their thirst for blood had not been satisfied. Their hope to accuse the woman and trap the One they saw as their rival was dashed. They slunk away defeated. Jesus had had the last word!

This unnamed woman was left alone with Jesus. She was still guilty, but this is where true love is clearly visible. What she had been

---

9   John 8:6
10 John 8:6
11 Psalm 103:14
12 John 8:7

seeking was clearly seen here, as she stood fully exposed in the dirt and the shame. Perfect love was right before her. Jesus stood back up. When no one else would stand up for her, Jesus stood up and looked at her face-to-face. He spoke to her heart to heart. He said, "Woman, where are those accusers of yours?"[13]

He said, "Look around. You have nothing to fear or be ashamed of in My Presence!" He called her woman. The word *woman* in Greek means "My lady, my bride"![14] This time, she is identified by Jesus, not by her sin but as His own.

He asks us the same question. "Who is worthy to accuse you? Is anyone perfect enough to cast the first stone when you are in My presence? Do you accuse yourself? Even *you* are not qualified to accuse yourself in My presence. I have come to bear your sin and shame. If I have taken it from you, why would you take it back? Are you more powerful that I? Are you more worthy than I? Silence the accusers in your head with My truth. Hear My voice over that of the accuser."

Jesus then says to the woman, "Neither do I condemn you; go and sin no more."[15]

She heard Jesus's voice of pardon. His voice of perfect love. He neither accused her nor excused her. She was guilty, but He came to bring mercy. He would not give her what she deserved. He came to cancel the death she deserved. He came to pay the price to give her what she didn't deserve, His grace, another chance to get it right. Aren't you grateful for another chance? God says He will never remember our sin.[16] All our chances are second chances.

The meaning of the word *remember*[17] is not in the forgetful sense. The thought of having a forgetful God is concerning to me. He remembers our sin no more in that He does not call it to mind when we repeatedly come before Him with the same mistake. He doesn't use it against us or apply it to our account as debt. That's

[13] John 8:10
[14] Strong's concordance #1135, GUNE
[15] John 8:11
[16] Jeremiah 31:34; Hebrews 8:12
[17] Strong's concordance #2142, ZAKAR; #3403, MIMNESKO

why we cannot forgive and forget. We remember but the question is, will we use it against the one we have forgiven? Will we dig up old offenses to use as present-day ammunition? With Jesus, we are forgiven. Our debt is cancelled. We are no longer condemned.

We can never outspend His mercy and grace. The woman came expecting her own funeral but left with a new life. She came as a woman condemned and left as the bride of Christ. She was now His beloved, rescued to be set apart for Him. She found the love for which she was really searching. She found her knight in shining armor dressed as a Lamb for the slaughter, but she knew Him by His love for her. She was His. Instead of working to earn love, she could now love out of the wellspring of love she had found in Jesus. His love is enough!

Scripture doesn't give us a follow up story on this woman. I think it's because she is us. Each one of us is called to finish the story. What would Jesus write in the dirt but not speak audibly when we are accused? Will we hear His voice of love over the voice of the accuser? He has covered us with the blood of His sacrifice, making us perfectly acceptable to God and He is continually working to perfect us. His Word says, "For by one offering He has perfected forever those who are *being* sanctified."[18] We are a perfected work in progress. Will we go and sin no more, accepting His gift of forgiveness, accepting His rescue and His love in spite of who we know we are? When (not if) we do sin, will we come fully exposed at His feet and allow Him to cover us again with His mercy and grace? Will we be willing to keep going and sin no more or will we stay in an ash heap of shame and accusation.

He invites us: "Let us therefore come boldly to the throne of grace, that we may obtain mercy and find grace to help in time of need."[19]

Our greatest need is when we realize we are guilty, we have no excuse, and we have no way of escape. We are bankrupt and in desperate need. Will we be afraid of Jesus, or will our only fear be

---

[18] Hebrews 10:14 (emphasis added)
[19] Hebrews 4:16

of offending and displeasing Him? Will we turn from the One Who knows all our secrets and loves us anyway? Will our only fear be of being left without Him? We know that He will never desert us or forsake (abandon) us. When everyone else leaves us in the dirt, He is there, not to accuse or excuse but to lift us up and set us on the road again with Him. Will we follow Him, or will we continue to be distracted by the allure of false lovers? He has shown us His pure and genuine love, the perfect love of the Father. He admonishes us to go and sin no more. He cautions us to not get caught up in the alluring traps of love that lead to destruction. As we fix our eyes on Him, we can know intimately what true love is. The search will be over.

Jesus says this: "I have loved you and will continue to love you with My perfect love. My love does not change with moods or circumstances. You can lean hard on My love, and it will never give way. Human love is not like that. It cannot bear the weight apart from Me. You can find great love in another but never perfect love. And My perfect love will never be taken from you by death. It will never walk away from you. It will never trick you or deceive you. Do not idealize or idolize any other love. Only My love is real and everlasting."

Paul's letter to the Romans tells us, "Who then will condemn us? Will Christ? No! For He is the One who died for us and came back to life again for us and is sitting at the place of highest honor next to God, pleading for us there in heaven."[20]

We do not have to live in a place of condemnation, of poor performance reviews, of the shame of widowhood or single parenting. We do not have to live alone and unloved no matter our circumstances.

Jesus has had the last word. He is seated as the final authority. He is in heaven right now pleading our case. We can confidently go and live as the disciple who Jesus loves. I don't need to compare or compete. I don't need to judge or jockey for first position. I am not a candidate for His love. I am the object of His love.[21] And so are you!

---

[20] Romans 8:34 TLB
[21] Christine Caine, *Don't Look Back* (Caso Writing LLC, Nelson Books, 2023).

Each one of us is one of a kind to Him. His love is specific to each of us. His love is what identifies us as His own and what attracts others to Him.

John, the disciple Jesus loved, wrote us these words spoken by Jesus: "And so I am giving a new commandment to you now—love each other just as much as I love you. Your strong love for each other will prove to the world that you are My disciples."[22]

His love is our gift and our mission. It's from Him and for Him. We can live from a place of being loved, not to earn love. So go, my friends, as a perfected work in progress and live loved!

---

[22] John 13:34–35 TLB

CHAPTER 15

Distortions

We saw in John 8 that the love that God intends is His perfect love that continually perfects us.[1] We are a perfected work in progress. We are His and He continues to make us more and more His. We saw how Jesus broke through the barriers that the Pharisees had created that distorted His love. We saw how Jesus tore down the walls that the woman herself had created by her own misguided pursuit of love. It doesn't matter what we do or what someone does to us, God will always break through for those who seek to follow Him. The lack that we may perceive is never a lack in His love. The lack is always in our ability to receive it.

Such was the case for me, even after I had been pursuing and following the Lord for over ten years. You see, we can have head knowledge of His truth and still be lacking in heart belief that changes the way we act. Our head knowledge must drop into our heart if we are to walk in wholehearted devotion.

My family of origin was not a demonstrative one. Rarely, if ever, were the words "I love you" spoken. Physical affection was scarce. Because my family was ravaged by alcoholism, we presented a beautiful exterior while masking the damage within. No family is perfect and many that I know have had similar experiences. The walls we

---

[1]   Hebrews 10:14

build to protect ourselves may seem to be effective for the short term, but they also create barriers and walls that distort God's truth.

Even before the suicide death of my father, I was hesitant to speak the word *father*. After that experience, I was unable to speak or even think about it without a seriously repulsive internal response. In spite of that, God showed me that He still intended that I honor my father and that I forgive him…again and again. This was not for my father's sake but for mine. The bitterness and anger that I was harboring was eating away at me and my relationship with my Heavenly Father. Very soon after my father's death, God showed me that I was to honor my father by leading worship at his graveside burial. I argued vehemently, but being in a state of shock and desperation, I chose to obey out of sheer desire to please God, Who was and still is my only hope. There was no other way. I see now how that was the beginning of the walls being torn down between me and my heavenly Father.

Shortly thereafter, in my anger and confusion that ensued, I sought counsel with two trusted friends. They prayed for me and with me. They prayed that I would climb up in the lap of my Heavenly Father to receive His comfort. This image crashed in on me and stopped me dead in my tracks. I was filled with fear. This was not the reverential fear that God intends in response to His power and holiness. This was the dreadful, run-for-your-life kind of fear. I was unable to continue with them in prayer. I explained to my friends that I could never climb up on His lap. I was terrified that He would refuse me. I feared that He would get up, dump me off, walk away and abandon me. I was too afraid. I had been hurt and ambushed too many times to open myself up again to that kind of rejection.

My friends and I sat quietly while I wrestled with my thoughts. I knew that my reaction was not based on the truth of His Word, but I also knew I couldn't allow myself to climb up in His lap. Knowing me better than I know myself, God gave me a picture in my mind that day that has been imprinted on my heart ever since. I literally saw my Heavenly Father get off His throne and sit on the floor with me. I couldn't come to Him, but He was more than willing to come down to me. This was such a tremendous breakthrough for me. I was seeing the truth of Who He really is and not the distorted picture that my earthly experience had created. God was not the stone-cold statue to whom I had prayed. He was not the unpredictable, controlling deity that I had imagined. His were not deaf ears on which my rote prayers and vain repetitions had fallen. He was a living, caring loving Father God Who wanted me to be with Him.

I had created my Father God in my own image, according to my experience instead of seeing Him in the light of His truth. I had repeatedly read the words about Who He is in His Word, but I was never able to really actually apply them and experience Him because of the barriers and walls I had built. I had put God in my own neat, safe, little box; but He wasn't about to stay there. He wanted me to know Him intimately as more than "Father." He wanted me to know Him as "Abba,"[2] Daddy, as His beloved child.

This was such a personal and intimate revelation to me. As Mary, I still ponder it and treasure it in my heart.[3] The revelation was so intimate to me that it took time for me to make the correlation that the Father has sent His Son, Jesus to show me His love. Jesus agreed to leave His throne in heaven to come down to literally sit with me in my low position and squalid condition on earth just to show me how much the Father loved me. Jesus came down to *be* true love for me. That was the love that the Father intended. The lack I had perceived was not in His provision but in my own distorted perception.

I have recently seen another example of the tender love of God. Peter denied Jesus three times,[4] just as Jesus had predicted.[5] Even before Peter fell, Jesus told Peter that He prayed for him so that his faith would not fail.[6] Jesus then told Peter that *when* (not if) he returned to Him, to strengthen his brothers. Jesus would not waste Peter's failure.

---

2   Strong's concordance #5, ABBA
3   Luke 2:19
4   John 18:27
5   Luke 22:34
6   Luke 22:32

After His resurrection, Jesus finds Peter fishing.[7] Jesus invites him to breakfast at the shore around a coal fire, reminiscent of the fire around which Peter had denied Jesus. Three times Jesus asks Peter if he loved Him, reminiscent of the number of times that Peter denied Jesus. The best part, however, is knowing the meaning of the words used for love in this account. In the original Greek, the first two times Jesus asks Peter if he loves Him, He uses the word *agapao*.[8] Agape love is the divine, sacrificial, perfect, unconditional love of God. Peter answers that he loves Jesus, using another Greek word for love, *phileo*.[9] Phileo love is a friendship kind of love. In essence, Peter is admitting that the love he has for Jesus is not the love to which Jesus is referring. Peter could not reach the height of the love that Jesus intended. Jesus, however, still told Peter to do His work of feeding and shepherding the sheep. But the third time that Jesus questions Peter about his love, He says, "Do you *phileo*[10] Me?" Jesus knew that Peter could not reach the height of "agape" love so He asked Peter if he could "phileo" Him. Jesus came down to Peter's ability to love to meet him right where he was. He would certainly take him higher, but Jesus came down to Peter's level to bring him along. It doesn't matter where we are, God will meet us there and carry us up to Him. Now, that's *agape*!

We are created in the image of God.[11] God is love.[12] So we are created to grow and thrive in His love. Adam and Eve had perfect communion with God in the Garden of Eden until sin entered. Sin broke communion with God. God had to maintain the standard of His holiness. He could not wink at their sin and rebellion and still be holy. God needed to send them away, but they were not without provision. Remember that God created the animals that He would require for the sacrifice for sin before He even created man. God allowed Adam and Eve to choose to disobey Him. He did not want

---

[7] John 21:1–19
[8] Strong's concordance #25, AGAPAO
[9] Strong's concordance #5368, PHILEO
[10] John 21:17
[11] Genesis 1:27
[12] 1 John 4:16

robots. He wanted those He created to love Him willingly. Man sinned and man has been paying the price for sin ever since. We had been separated from our holy God because of that sin. That is, until the Father sent Jesus to reverse the curse of sin. It is, however, still a choice to receive the free gift of His love in Jesus. But Jesus is the only way back to communion with the Father. Jesus is the One Who restored our fellowship with the Father, and we must come only through Him.

Because of the presence of sin in the world, our experiences distort the truth. Satan is a liar and the father of lies.[13] He has been lying to us since he slithered into the Garden of Eden. He continually tries to distort the truth of God's Word, placing doubt in our thoughts. "Did God really say…?"[14] God tells us to renew our minds, to be transformed in our thinking so that we can know His will, so we will know for sure Who He really is and what He desires for us.[15] For me, this took years of pouring over the truth until the light of transformation shone through that day in prayer. The prison of my own making was opening. I wish I could say that I ran out and fully embraced all that God had for me. The truth is, I was still reluctant to let His truth be my guide instead of being led by my history. I had wandered in the wilderness for many years and God had to bring me to a place of decision like He brought Moses in the wilderness.

"You have circled this mountain long enough; turn to the north."[16]

Until I allow God's Word and not my experience to be my true north, I will continue to be lost, disoriented, and misguided. Until I allow Him to be my place of security and the place in which I can pin my trust, I will continue to be confused, deceived and full of fear. Until I believe that He is greater than what I had known so far and until I act out that belief, I will continue to circle the same mountain in the same desert.

---

13 John 8:44
14 Genesis 3:1
15 Romans 12:2
16 Deuteronomy 2:3

Truth had been distorted by what had been done to me and by what I had done. Just as Eve sinned by taking satan's temptation bait regarding the forbidden fruit. Just as Adam sinned by listening to Eve instead of obeying the Father, I had been listening to lies in my thoughts for so long. "Did God really say He would never leave you? Did He really say His love was freely given and you didn't need to perform to earn it? Did He really say to come just as you are and not wait until you clean up your act?" My internal dialogue was not in alignment with the truth. Instead of declaring the truth, I was engaging with the devil's lies, just as Eve did. She had not accurately recalled the truth of what God said to her. Instead, she questioned it and added to it. God said that they could freely eat of every tree in the garden except the tree of the knowledge of good and evil.[17] Eve told the serpent they could not eat it *or* touch it. She had added an unnecessary restriction and allowed the serpent to deceive her.

Through the picture that God gave me during that prayer, I was able to begin settling the issue of the love of my Heavenly Father. He was true to His Word. My Heavenly Father had demonstrated His love for me in that while I was still far from Him, Christ came down from His throne in heaven and died for me.[18] I am not just one of the herd. He knows my name.[19] He stepped down for me...and you.

This breakthrough was only one of many treasures that I have experienced as He continues to tear down the walls that I have built to protect myself. I have had many other experiences where I was lost and disoriented. God has continued to give one revelation after another, break down one wall after another, illuminate one shadow after another to reveal His treasures as He continues to perfect me. He lifts off the weight that so easily encumbers and clears out the sin that so easily entangles.[20] He made me His when I asked Him to be my Lord. He continually makes me more and more His as I allow Him to break down the barriers that separate us.

---

[17] Genesis 2: 16–17
[18] Romans 5:8
[19] John 10:3
[20] Hebrews 12:1

In the "meantime," time will be mean. So what am I supposed to do? I am supposed to be "sober and vigilant,"[21] not deceived and deluded like Adam and Eve were in the garden. I am to trust Him for every provision. I am to rest in the assurance that after I have "suffered a while (He will), perfect, establish, strengthen, and settle me."[22] I must remember that He is praying for me[23] that my faith will not fail. I can stop squirming and trying to get my own way. I can stop trying to hide and protect myself. I can come to Him honestly, knowing that He will never reject me as long as I am pursuing Him. I can climb up in His lap for His perfect care. He can be trusted. And after I have returned to Him and His truth, after He has unearthed His treasures, I can strengthen my brothers and sisters by my testimony of His unfailing faithfulness, even in my faithlessness.[24]

> Lord, thank You for this truth:
> There's no shadow You won't light up
> Mountain You won't climb up
> Coming after me
> There's no wall You won't kick down
> Lie You won't tear down
> Coming after me.[25]

> Where can I go from Your Spirit?
> Or where can I flee from Your presence?
> If I say, "Surely the darkness shall fall on me,"
> Even the night shall be light about me;
> Indeed, the darkness shall not hide from You,
> But the night shines as the day;
> The darkness and the light are both alike to You.[26]

---

[21] 1 Peter 5:8
[22] 1 Peter 5:10
[23] Hebrews 7:25
[24] 2 Timothy 2:13
[25] Cory Asbury, *Reckless Love*.
[26] Psalm 139:7, 11, 12

CHAPTER 16

Born into Thorns

God created a perfect world in the Garden of Eden. He called it good.[1] Then God created man, male and female in His likeness.[2] He called it very good.[3] God provided, not just one but an abundance of trees with fruit that was good and for them to freely eat. There was only one restriction: The tree of the knowledge of good and evil was off limits because the consequence of eating from it was death.

Life was good. Paradise actually. The Greek word for *paradise*, *paradeisos*, means garden.[4] When I look at that word, I see "para" or surrounded by and "deisos," God. Surrounded by God! That is not the official translation, but it sure paints a beautiful picture for me.

Then the serpent slithered in. He crawled in with a distortion of the truth and an offer of sin. The original instruction to Adam was not to eat of the tree,[5] period. Eve misquoted the instruction to include the prohibition to not even touch the tree.[6] Somehow the truth had been distorted and trouble began. Satan, the serpent, questioned God's Word and introduced the option of being their own

---

[1] Genesis 1:25
[2] Genesis 1:27
[3] Genesis 1:31
[4] Strong's concordance #3857, PARADEISOS, from Luke 23:43
[5] Genesis 2:17
[6] Genesis 3:2

god. Satan's intent has always been to destroy the perfect fellowship that God desires with man. In His loving sovereignty, God allows man to have free will. He wants us to come to Him willingly, out of love, not mechanically out of compulsion. He wants children who obey Him out of honor and reverence, not out of fear of destruction.

In just three short chapters of the Bible, God's perfect creation is marred by sin. The rest of the forty-seven chapters of Genesis and the sixty-five books of the Bible that follow are God's way of restoring fellowship with His children. His ultimate desire is to be with us. The decision that Adam and Eve made to partner with evil has forever tainted our heritage. We are born into that sin. Scripture says that the one man's (Adam's) sin spread to all men causing death.[7] Sin is a congenital, contagious, fatal disease that we all must reconcile. We all have sinned and fall short of the glory that God intended.[8]

Sin slithered into the picture, and God pronounced His judgment. Woman would experience pain in childbirth and man would have to toil for their sustenance. Both would experience death. The thorns that grow in the garden[9] are the fruit of sin, the consequence of disobedience. The thorns of sin are the reason for all the pain that we experience. God does not give us rules just to exercise His authority but to demonstrate His love for us. He knows, intimately, how harmful and destructive sin is to us. His desire is not to control us but to protect us. But Adam and Eve were deceived. They considered the question posed by the serpent, "Did God *really* say…"[10] They chose deception over truth. As a result of their disobedience, they both were cast out of the Garden. Another tree in the Garden was the Tree of Life. If Adam and Eve had been allowed to stay in the Garden, they would have lived eternally in the sin that they had chosen. Their banishment was not to punish them but to protect them and us until a Savior would rescue us from eternal sin.

We still, however, experience the thorns of sin. If you have ever given birth, you know the pain of birthing another thorny human

---

[7] Romans 5:12
[8] Romans 3:23
[9] Genesis 3:18
[10] Genesis 3:1

being. If you have ever parented or provided care to a child for more than ten minutes, you understand the thorniness of sin. An infant is completely and totally self-centered. Nothing else in the universe exists outside of themselves. You don't need to teach a toddler to declare, "Mine!" nor do you need to teach them to say, "No!" These are all external manifestations of the internal sin nature. Sin is completely and totally self-centered. Learning other-centeredness is a steep learning curve. Let's get real. Just look in the mirror and you can see remnants of that even into adulthood. It is only when we look into the mirror of God's Word that we can begin to be healed and transformed. The mirror of comparison with others is distorted. The mirror of our culture is completely clouded. The only reliable mirror is found in the example of the perfection of Jesus Christ, God in the flesh.

So we are born into the thorns and carry them with us. Enter Jesus, born into our thorns as the only perfect Being. Jesus, in His perfection and sinless nature as God, is the only One who is able to pay the price to satisfy the wrath of our Holy God. God could not excuse our sin and still be a holy God. But Jesus, God in flesh, was willing and able to pay the price for our redemption so that we could be bought back from death and brought back into fellowship with God, in paradise,[11] surrounded by Him.

That Baby, born in a manger, came for the intended purpose to die for us on the cross. He was willing to endure not only the brutality of the cross but also the humiliation of the mockery and physical abuse on the way to the cross. And He endured it to save the very ones who were responsible for His abuse. On His way to our redemption, Jesus was crowned mockingly with a crown of thorns. Man thought that they had silenced Jesus as king. The enemy thought he had defeated Jesus and His purposes. But Jesus wore that crown of thorns willingly to reverse the curse that was created in the Garden of Eden.

One man sinned, and so death ruled all people because of that one man. But now some people accept God's full grace and the great gift of

---

[11] Luke 23:43

being made right with Him. They will surely have true life and rule through the one Man, Jesus Christ.[12]

Jesus came to restore our fellowship with our holy God. The only way we can enter into intimate communion with the Father is by accepting the work of Christ on the cross and His resurrection as He defeated death. We know that we cannot enter on our own merit. We have nothing to make ourselves holy before a holy God. We need a Savior. We believe that Jesus is the Son of God, the Messiah, sent to rescue us from the prison and slavery of sin's grip. We come to God the Father behind Jesus the Son. The Father sees us through Jesus's perfection.

Sometimes my children would bring friends home who I did not know. They, as strangers, were not welcomed in. But as my children introduced them to me as their friends, they were welcomed into our home. When we come to the Father, we must come as Christ's friends. We must present ourselves covered in the righteousness of Christ. When we believe Jesus is Who He says He is, He calls us His friend.[13] If we try to stand in our own righteousness, Scripture says we are covering ourselves with filthy rags.[14] In the Hebrew, that is translated as menstrual cloths.[15] We are disgusting to God as we present ourselves to Him on our own merit. The only merit that allows us access to the Father is the merit of Jesus Christ. He bore the thorns to take away our thorns. He endured the cross to defeat the consequence of the sin into which we were born.

In the garden after sinning, Adam and Eve attempted to cover themselves with fig leaves.[16] These were a flimsy, inadequate covering before their Holy God. But God Himself provided them with the skins of animal as covering for them.[17] God had created the animals that were necessary for the covering even before He created man. Before man needed the covering, God had provided it. God's ulti-

---

[12] Romans 5:17 International Children's Bible
[13] John 15:14
[14] Isaiah 64:6
[15] Strong's concordance #5713c, IDDAH
[16] Genesis 3:7
[17] Genesis 3:21

mate plan, in the fullness of time, was that His very own Son, God in human flesh, would provide the covering needed to enter into fellowship with God for eternity. Jesus is the only adequate covering and God has provided Him. Everything else is flimsy and inadequate. Our responsibility is to receive Him and to put Him on, to be clothed in Him.[18] We are to identify ourselves with Christ, look like Him, dress like Him, and make our outward appearance resemble Him and not our thorny flesh.

Thank You, Father, that You provided exactly what I needed from the foundation of the world. Thank You, Lord Jesus, for your obedience to the cross, enduring all that accompanied it. Thank You for Your Spirit that now indwells those of us who are Yours. We have accepted that we have no merit on our own. We are born into a sin nature that cannot present itself before a holy God. We know that it is only in You, Lord Jesus, that we can have communion with the Father here on earth and have an eternal home in heaven. Thank You, Lord Jesus, that You wore the crown of thorns. Thank You that You bore our sin and defeated the power of the serpent and sin. You stripped satan of his power and authority on the cross. It was there that You made a public spectacle[19] of him and his minions. The thorns no longer have power over me because of You.

> You were dead because of your sins and because your sinful nature was not yet cut away. Then God made you alive with Christ, for He forgave all our sins. He canceled the record of the charges against us and took it away by nailing it to the cross. In this way, He disarmed the spiritual rulers and authorities. He shamed them publicly by His victory over them on the cross. (Colossians 2:13–15 NLT)

---

[18] Romans 13:14
[19] Colossians 2:15 NIV

CHAPTER 17

From Thorns to Delight

Thorns are the result of sin as we have seen in the Garden of Eden.[1] They are the result of our attempts to be independent of God, our Creator. When we strike out on our own, we find ourselves in painful places. The journey back from pain and lament to restored fellowship with God requires acceptance of our need and submission to His ways. Then we can delight in Him and find renewed joy. Often, that journey is a long, steep and arduous one. It requires desperation, resolute determination, and a steadfast focus on the goal. We see that in the example of Jesus as He made the long, steep, arduous journey through the cross on our behalf.

Repeatedly, in His Word, God introduces us to His children who have found themselves in places of unrelenting pain. Their pain is the result of their own disobedience or the result of someone else's disobedience, inflicting pain on them. God allowed them, and even encouraged them, to give full voice to their lament. He welcomed their openness and honesty, as He does mine. He says to us, even today, to "pour out your heart before Him."[2] At the same time, He invites me to "taste and see that He is good."[3]

---

[1] Genesis 3:18
[2] Psalm 62:8
[3] Psalm 34:8

God told the prophet Ezekiel to speak His message to the rebellious house of Israel. It was God's message alone that could change the mourning and lamenting[4] His children were experiencing into sweetness.[5] He promises that my lament will *lead* to delight, not miraculously change into it, hence the long and arduous trek.

My circumstances may not change but something inside of me will need to change. The acidity of my soul will be neutralized by God's healing touch through prayer and His Word to perceive my circumstances in a new and life-changing way. It will require me to admit that I have a need beyond myself and a submission on my part with the goal of being like Jesus. When I know what my goal is, it brings renewed strength and clarity. Jesus learned obedience by the things He suffered.[6] He was not exempt from our trials and pains. He experienced them all in the flesh and His obedience to the Father secured deliverance and salvation for us.

The apostle Paul told us about his thorn.[7] The Greek translation for thorn is a sharp affliction producing pain.[8] Paul goes on to say that he delights, glories, and boasts with pleasure in his weaknesses so that the power of Christ would rest on him.[9] The word he uses for boast is this: "kauxáomai—properly, living with 'head up high,' boasting from a particular vantage point by having the right base of operation to deal successfully with a matter."[10]

Paul's perception of his weaknesses and thorns originated from the "right base of operation." He knew Who God is, and he knew who he was in God. The result of this kind of perception is explained in the Amplified Bible: "that the strength and power of Christ (the Messiah) may rest (yes, may pitch a tent over and dwell) upon me!"

As I delight in my hardships, difficulties, and weaknesses my focus is changed to a higher place in Christ, a right base of oper-

---

[4] Ezekiel 2:10

[5] Ezekiel 3:3

[6] Hebrews 5:8

[7] 2 Corinthians 12:7

[8] Strong's concordance #4647, SKOLOPS

[9] 2 Corinthians 12:9–10

[10] Strong's concordance #2744

ation. As I shift my focus from me to Him, I am encompassed by the strength and power of Almighty God. He will pitch His tent of protection and provision over me, and I will dwell in His sanctuary. That is reason to boast! It does not happen right away, but it is the promise to which I can stake my claim.

That change of focus is described frequently by David in his psalms. He pours out his heart and speaks his lament freely. Then, in the culmination of his lament, he declares, "But, God." David, Paul, John, Job, Jeremiah, and many more of the saints learned to change their place of habitation from the earth-bound focus to the freedom and abundance of the heavenlies, seated with Christ,[11] in a new place at His throne of grace, seeing from His vantage point, the right base of operation.

I originally started to write this chapter less than a year after Ernie's death. I could see the insurmountable task before me was to change my focus from myself to God. I needed to find a new place in God, a place of deliverance and salvation from the oppression of grief and loneliness and fear. Since then, through reading His Word and talking and listening to Him in prayer, God has repeatedly caused me to fix my eyes on Him. This is where He has enabled me, not just allowed me but *enabled* me, to go on the heights.[12] He instructs me to lift up my eyes to the hills where my help comes from.[13] The Lord is the One Who helps me change my myopic focus from me to Him. Without Him, I am so consumed with the present and the lack that I perceive, I cannot see the future and the riches He has promised. I cannot see the forest for the trees, the bigger picture. But God has caused me to sing the song of ascents, the songs of trust that God is able and willing to enable me to ascend to that higher place of knowing Him and of praise and worship.

Psalms 120 to 134 are known as the psalms of ascent. Jewish pilgrims would sing them as they made the arduous trip up Mt. Zion to the temple in Jerusalem. The ascent was necessary for them to

---

[11] Ephesians 2:6
[12] Habakkuk 3:19
[13] Psalm 121:1

be able to worship at the great Jewish festivals. By singing God's Word, they were encouraged and strengthened for the journey. They shifted their focus from the weariness of the trek to the truth of their God and the joy of celebrating His goodness at Passover, the Feast of Tabernacles, and Pentecost.

My ascent over the last almost two decades has been a long, uphill, arduous journey with many setbacks and advances. I still learn daily from the Word of God. Jesus, Himself, showed me how to make that ascent when He was in the garden of Gethsemane. That was the place of the olive press, the place of crushing. Though He was facing intense humiliation and a brutal crucifixion, Jesus chose, "Nevertheless, not My will but Yours be done."[14] Jesus's focus was to glorify His Father and to bring glory to His name. His goal was to bring us from the Garden of Gethsemane back to the Garden of Eden, in restored fellowship with God.

As I continue on this life-long journey, often uphill, I am able to gradually come to new places of acceptance and submission when I am faced with trials. I may even come to a place to be able to boast or delight in them even as I don't understand them. David stated my case when he admitted: "When I considered how to understand this, it was too great an effort for me and too painful."[15]

Trying to understand causes weariness and is a burden way too heavy for me to carry. Like Job, I speak of things, and I try to understand things way too wonderful for me.[16] Not wonderful in the delightful and pleasing sense, but wonderful in the Hebrew *pala*[17] sense. That is, beyond the bounds of human power, expectation, or comprehension. Simply stated, it is a match between my three-pound brain and an infinite God. There is no contest there, and He is worthy to be trusted in the trials. As I trust Him, I allow Him to exhibit His capable and matchless care instead of trying to make it on my own.

---

[14] Luke 22:42
[15] Psalm 73:16 AMP
[16] Job 42:3
[17] Strong's Concordance #6381, PALA

In the book of Job, we see where Job was stripped completely of all his earthly treasures. He became a broken man and was incapable of understanding. His friends, despite their best efforts and intentions, were also unable to understand. Job had no ability to change anything that happened to Him. All he could do was change his perspective. In His brokenness, in His profound spiritual bankruptcy, abiding in the dust and ashes of his pain and misery, he called out in honesty to God. When the distracting voices of man and his own flurry of questions were finally silenced, the dust cleared and the clouds parted. God spoke: "Who is this who darkens counsel by words without knowledge?

Now prepare yourself like a man; I will question you, and you shall answer Me."[18]

Now, that is a clear delineation between Creator and created! After thirty-eight chapters of questions and human reasoning, Job finally got to the place of humility that David had found:

> Therefore I have uttered what I did not
>   understand,
> Things too wonderful for me, which I did not
>   know.
> Listen, please, and let me speak;
> You said, "I will question you, and you shall
>   answer Me."
>
> I have heard of You by the hearing of the ear,
> But now my eye sees You.
> Therefore I abhor myself,
> And repent in dust and ashes.[19]

Job got a revelation of God in His glory. He realized that he had heard much about God. But now, His eyes had seen God. Like

---

[18] Job 38:2–3
[19] Job 42:3–6

Moses,[20] Job had seen God face-to-face and God spoke to him. Job heard and saw up close and personal. It was an undeniable encounter. Perhaps Job did not actually see God in the optical sense, but he did see Him in Hebrew *raah*[21] sense, in the perceiving, understanding, and experiential sense. He had come to know God in a much more intimate way. He now knew God in a Hebrew *yada*[22] way, as a man knows his wife.

And what did that intimacy cause? It caused him to despise himself and it caused him to repent.[23] It caused even more brokenness. Oh, how my flaws are magnified in the presence of the perfection of God. I am made painfully more aware of my inadequacies and imperfections as I am fully exposed before Him and as He reveals Himself to me.

My brokenness leaves me with two options. I can turn and run away. I can hide and break fellowship with Him, thereby forfeiting and rejecting the greatest treasure I have ever known, or I can admit my imperfections, failures, and shortcomings. I can agree with God that I, indeed, fall short of His expectations.[24] I can confess that my shortcomings are not pleasing or attractive to Him. I can ask Him to forgive me and correct me. Then I can press into Him with all that I am and with all that He has made me to be. As I face my flaws and my humanity and repent, I turn from my world to His.

It is His kindness that leads me to repentance.[25] It is knowing His goodness that makes me want to be corrected instead of run. It is not fear of punishment but a fear of displeasing Him. It is an intense desire to do and be all that He desires. Then I can enter His sanctuary.[26] I can enter that secret place of life with God, the right base of operation, right here on earth in the midst of my pain. It begins with trust, even in my lack of understanding.

---

20 Exodus 33:11
21 Strong's concordance #7200, RAAH
22 Strong's concordance #3045, YADA
23 Job 42:6
24 Romans 3:23
25 Romans 2:4
26 Psalm 73:17

He is my Shepherd. I am His sheep. I must trust Him to lead me to rest. I could strike out on my own in search of rest, but I will quickly wear myself out on the journey. I won't have the power or protection for the quest. As I stick close to him and follow His instruction in His Word, I find perfect care. Even when the road is rocky and narrow on the ascent up the mountain, He will keep me safe. He promised.

It is in His sanctuary, in the place where He is, that I can gradually gain His understanding. As I earnestly seek Him, desperately thirst and long for Him and require Him as my vital necessity,[27] I behold His power and His glory. I experience His love that is even better than life, and I am satisfied with His riches.[28] His riches don't merely pacify for the moment like worldly treasures. His riches satisfy and bring an end to longing. I must lay aside my desires and expectations for worldly satisfaction in exchange for His desires. In that right base of operation, seated with Him, I can find contentment and His sweetness in the thorns of this world.

No, the journey is not an easy one. In fact, ease will lull me into a satisfaction that hinders my desire for the "higher place." The thorns are what prod me on to the ascent. With His enabling, I will go on the heights. Even when everything around me is barren, I will find satisfaction and rest in Him alone. Therein lies the delight[29] to which Paul referred.

God says, *"Delight yourself also in the LORD, And He shall give you the desires of your heart."*[30]

The original word for delight means to be soft and pliable.[31] When I am rigidly adhering to my own desires, I miss the desires of His heart that He has for me. My delight cannot be in what I desire but it must be in what He desires for me. There are many times when I thought I knew what I desired, but it would have been more harmful for me in the end. I am grateful that He hasn't given

---

[27] Jeremiah 29:13 AMPC
[28] Psalm 63:1–5
[29] 2 Corinthians 12:10 NIV
[30] Psalm 37:4
[31] Strong's concordance #6026, ANOG

me all the things for which I have prayed! When I delight in Him, I become more pliable, more open to His lead. Then He will give me what He desires for me and not the carnal things that I desire. That is delightful!

It has, obviously, taken me a long hard climb to find delight in losing the love of my life. *But God* is faithful. It's not that I have found delight in the loss, but I have found delight in all the treasures He has given me to restore the years the locusts have eaten.[32] There is a song that expresses this journey for me. It is "Lead On Good Shepherd" by Patrick Mayberry. In the chorus, it says, "There ain't nothing sweeter than to watch You make a way." That is exactly what God has done for me to lead me in His way. In the thorns, where there seemed to be no way, He made a way, a road in the wilderness and streams in the desert.[33] He is my promised Waymaker.

Lord, thank You for leading me through the valley of the shadow of death. Thank You for keeping me safe on the ascent. Thank You that, when I stray, I am never out of Your sight or reach. Thank You that Your goodness and mercy chase after and pursue me all the days of my life[34] until I am home safely with You.

> But now, thus says the LORD, who created you, O
>   Jacob (Cindy),
> And He who formed you, O Israel (Cindy):
> "Fear not, for I have redeemed you;
> I have called you by your name;
> You are Mine.
> When you pass through the waters, I will be with
>   you;
> And through the rivers, they shall not overflow
>   you.

---

[32] Joel 2:25
[33] Isaiah 43:19
[34] Psalm 23:6

When you walk through the fire, you shall not
    be burned,
Nor shall the flame scorch you.
For I am the LORD your God. (Isaiah 43:1–3)

    For I am persuaded that neither death nor
life, nor angels nor principalities nor powers, nor
things present nor things to come, nor height nor
depth, nor any other created thing, shall be able
to separate us from the love of God which is in
Christ Jesus. (Romans 8:38–39)

PART 4

Treasures in Waiting

But those who wait on the LORD
Shall renew their strength;
They shall mount up with wings like eagles,
They shall run and not be weary,
They shall walk and not faint.

—Isaiah 40:31

CHAPTER 18

Urgency in the Darkness

In my previous book, *A Walk Through the Shadow*, you can read about the details of my beloved husband Ernie's journey through cancer treatment. As he got more involved in treatment, the road got darker and more winding. We often felt lost and alone. In the fullness of God's timing, the insurance company provided us with a case manager. Her name was Jeanette, and she was one of the most informed and supportive members of the medical team. Her job was to oversee Ernie's entire treatment, to know about all the referrals and of course, to make sure all the bills would be paid. She also took it unto herself to offer much needed advice and emotional support. She always went above and beyond what was required of her to ensure our best possible outcome. She not only cared for Ernie; she knew how important it was for him to make sure I was provided for on our travels as well.

Before she was added to the team, it seemed that Ernie's treatments were not well coordinated. Ernie was being treated with still-experimental Interleukin II at Dartmouth Hitchcock Medical Center in New Hampshire. This treatment protocol required that Ernie be hospitalized for one week at a time in their hematology-oncology intensive care unit to receive intravenous infusions. He would then have one or two weeks off to recover and then be rehospitalized for another week of treatment. That constituted one "round" of treatment. The plan was that he would be treated with numerous rounds, four to six weeks apart. His PET scan results would determine if the treatment was working. After each round, we would wait to hear what the PET scan revealed to schedule another round.

The Interleukin II treatment caused harsh affects to Ernie's kidneys and blood pressure. It also caused intense shaking episodes called "rigors." These were treated with Demerol, which caused severe vomiting. In short, these were brutal sessions. I hope and pray that this treatment has become a little more humane since the testing phase. Always the optimist, when Ernie was asked what he did for a living in this phase of his life, he would say he was "in research"! In summary, it was a time of treatment for which we both needed to be prepared, repeatedly. I was committed to staying with Ernie in the ICU for the treatments due to the very high risks of medical complications. We also needed to make arrangements for our two children still at home, one with intensive special needs.

After one of these rounds, we were waiting and waiting for the results of Ernie's latest PET scan. According to the treatment protocol, Ernie was due for another round. We were anxious to begin making arrangements. I had taken a family leave from my part-time nursing position, and my leave was due to run out. Ernie was always the patient one. I, on the other hand, was headed toward a full-blown panic. Oh, me of little faith. I still confess to being a recovering control freak.

It was near Christmas. I called repeatedly to get answers. Each time I would be promised an answer by a certain deadline. Each time that deadline would come and go without an answer. Being a nurse, I vowed that I would never treat my patients' families like that. I was certain that someone needed to be informed about the run around that we were facing. Cancer is a very difficult and uncertain disease to live with in the first place. "They" were just making our lives more difficult and more uncertain. How cruel!

I sat down and wrote a letter to the two attending physicians at Dartmouth, copying to patient relations and Ernie's attending physician in Burlington, Vermont, who had made the initial referral. I tried to state our case as objectively as possible, attempting to keep my raging emotions at bay, at least on paper. The only response we got, initially, was from his doctor in Burlington. She was very understanding and compassionate, yet powerless to change our situation. It did feel better knowing that someone really did care. A few weeks later, we received a "letter" from patient relations, thanking us for sharing our concerns. I think it said something like, "it will be addressed in the order in which it was received." Not really, but that's what it felt like. I'm sure it ended up on the "pending shredding" pile, or the "blah, blah, blah whatever, tell us something that we *don't* know" pile. Sometimes I wonder why I bother. But thankfully, that's where Jeanette entered the picture to coordinate the increasing costs of Ernie's treatment. She was a gift from God. She confidently and completely arranged for all the treatment that was ahead and made sure we were both taken care of in the midst of it, even up to Ernie's death.

I think, at this point, I need to confess that, in this part of our journey, I'm not sure how truly dependent I was on prayer. I was in full-blown survival mode. I was frantically reaching for whatever strategies seemed available in the moment. I had forgotten God's past faithfulness, His present promises, and the secure future He had assured for both of us. It was much like David and the Ephod in a previous chapter. In spite of my forgetfulness and frantic activity, God knew what we needed, even before we asked.[1] He provided and strengthened our faith in the process. Will it remind me the next time I find myself in survival mode to stop and remember what He has taught me? Will I be trained by this experience or just endure it? Will it remind me of the proof of His faithfulness, even when I am faithless.[2]

I am so grateful that when I do pour out my heart to God, He hears immediately, He cares and He sends an answer. I may not "get" the answer right away, but I know that He is on it. It may not be the answer I wanted but He can be trusted to deliver His best for me.

"Pour out your hearts to Him, for God is our refuge. Selah" (Psalm 62:8b).

---

[1] Matthew 6:8
[2] 2 Timothy 2:13

Selah, in the original language, means to pause and calmly think about that. It is the brakes in an emotionally charged situation that causes me to know from whence comes my help.[3] Yes, the same God who created heaven and earth is on stand-by waiting to help me. I need to remember to "selah."

I am so grateful that God answers my plea as priority, no matter the order in which it was received. I am grateful that I will never hear these things when I pray:

* We're sorry; your prayer could not be completed as prayed. Please check your Handbook and try again later.
* If this is a real emergency, please hang up and dial 911 (call someone who can *really* help).
* Thank you for praying. All our representatives are busy with other prayers. Please hold for the next available prayer representative.
* We're sorry; the God you have reached is out of service at this time. No further information is available.
* Thank you for holding. Your prayer is very important to us. Please stay in prayer and you will be answered as soon as God is available.
* Do you have an appointment? A co-pay? A referral?
* You're cutting out. Can you hear Me now?
* Hello. This is God's secretary. Would you like His voice mail?
* Please leave a message after the beep.
* Please press 1 for God the Father, 2 for Jesus the Son, or 3 for the Holy Spirit.
* There will be an extra charge for this prayer considering the depths from which you are calling.
* Thank you for your prayer. We understand that you are in a difficult situation and we will do our best to address it... someday.

---

[3] Psalm 121:2

✳ All our representatives are busy with other callers. Please try our website at wedontwanttotalktoyourightnow.com

No. I hear, "Come right in, enter with confidence, and make yourself at home at the throne of grace. I have been waiting for you to come."[4]

God's phone number: Jeremiah 33:3, keeping it simple: "Call to Me, and I will answer you, and show you great and mighty things, which you do not know.

Call Him and He will answer you.[5] No caller ID necessary. He knows it's you before you call.[6]

"He (Jesus) ALWAYS lives to intercede for them (us)"[7] (emphasis and inserts added).

His line is always open, and I have heard that He answers knee-mail!

I have had many, many more opportunities for God to prove His faithfulness to me since Ernie's illness. I'd like to say I learned well from my initial experiences, that I have been trained by them. The truth is, I may not be a quick study, but I serve a faithful and long-suffering, patient God. He is my only answer.

Lord, please help me to "selah" Your words the next time my life is out of control and no one has an answer.

---

[4] Hebrews 4:16
[5] Jeremiah 33:3
[6] Isaiah 65:24
[7] Hebrews 7:25b

CHAPTER 19

What's Ahead?

The skill of waiting, as you have seen, is not my strong suit. To wait patiently continues to take years of training. Waiting in line, waiting my turn, waiting for this dinosaur of a computer to keep up with the flurry of my thoughts to get them on paper before I lose them, waiting for an answer, waiting on hold, knowing my call is very important to someone! In this world of instant gratification, we have lost the ability to wait. I often give up easily and look for more productive ways. Waiting suggests expectation. We wait on the phone expecting that someone is on the other end...somewhere. We wait for a bus with the full expectation that it will come...eventually. You have already seen how my expectations have sometimes misled me, but we can learn to wait expectantly without our own expectations. We can wait, trusting that God knows best.

In the Greek, the word that Apostle Paul uses for expectation is *apokaradokia*.[1]

> apokaradokía (from 575 /apó, "away from"; kara, "the head"; and 1380 /dokéō, "thinking")—properly, thinking forward (literally with

---

[1] Philippians 1:20; Romans 8:19

head out-stretched), referring to eager, intense expectation, strained expectancy[2]

I love looking at word origins because they paint their own picture. In the above definition, we can see that to "expect" can mean not only straining your neck to see what is ahead but also getting "away from the head" or getting out of my own head while I expect! In my own understanding, I am very shortsighted. I can't see down the road or around the next curve, so I make up my own story. I like to see what's coming but God knows if I see the whole picture, I will be totally overwhelmed. I may jump ship and miss the treasure that He has waiting for me. He only shows me enough to get me to the next level of maturity. He knows the end from the beginning,[3] *and* He knows how to get me safely to the end without self-destructing.

God says,

> Trust in the LORD with all your heart,
> And lean not on your own understanding;
> In all your ways acknowledge Him,
> And He shall direct your paths.[4]

To acknowledge Him, in the Hebrew, is to know Him intimately.[5] It is not a head, intellectual, "dating" kind of knowledge. It is a heart, experiential, "living with Him" kind of knowledge. You never really know someone until you live with them, right? It may be a roommate, a spouse, or a child. When you live with them, you really know them. That's why Jesus says to "abide in Him and He in us."[6] I like the concept of abiding in Him. He is perfect. But the concept of Him abiding with me? That's another story. To let Him see all my secret stashes and hiding places is scary for me. But as we allow Him to see it all, we find freedom. We can be free to trust Him. We learn

---

[2] Strong's concordance #603, APOKARADOKIA
[3] Isaiah 46:10
[4] Proverbs 3:5–6
[5] Strong's concordance #3045, YADA
[6] John 15:4

that He is gentle and caring like He was with the woman caught in the act of adultery.[7] As we trust in Him, we find hope. In my darkest of days, the Scripture I turn to is this: "Hope deferred makes the heart sick, But when the desire comes, it is a tree of life."[8]

I recently experienced a relapse in grief that sent me into a year-long tailspin. After eighteen years of being "content" as a widow, I began to be discontent, unsettled, wanting to know if this was all there is. All the years of idealizing my marriage came to a head. The longer I have been a widow, the more perfect my marriage has become in my remembrance. All the hard times were forgotten, and it was all romance and happiness in my mind. I began to, not only idealize but idolize my marriage and yearn for the past to a point of not wanting to move forward. Like Lot's wife, I was looking longingly back and had become a human salt lick![9] I was stuck in the past and yearning for something that could not be brought back to life. My hope was deferred, and my heart was sick.

It may have been the catalyst to or the result of something I experienced that I thought would bring me renewed hope, but I found myself in deep grief and confusion. I thought that God had a plan for me that brought me great excitement. I thought I had heard His voice, and it was good. Unfortunately, I was leaning on my own understanding. I was writing my own story totally off script from what God intended. In the midst of this, one of my daughter's asked me, "Mom, if this doesn't work out like you had hoped, will you still believe and love God?" I assured her that I would always believe God and love Him, but I would forever question my ability to hear His voice. I carried on in that belief until one day I realized how offensive that was to God. It was like telling my best friend that I love them, but I will never believe another word they said! It was my hope and my version of the story that was misdirected, not His voice. He *had* placed a renewed hope in my heart. It was just not the hope on which I had hung my hat. I was the one who had misunderstood the hope. I

---

[7]   John 8:3–11
[8]   Proverbs 13:12
[9]   Genesis 19:26

was trying to birth His hope prematurely as I understood it. I needed to wait for Him to fulfill the hope He desired for me.

When the rubber meets the road, how do we get from hopes dashed to life and peace? How do we trade in our own understanding of what Jesus intended by "abundant life"?[10] The life I was living was far from abundant, in my own perception. It took many months of wrestling with God and begging Him to change the desires of my heart. Pleading for Him to remove my own unrequited desire for His desires.

In the birth process of labor, a period of transition is reached. The process of birthing is well underway, and the promise is within sight, but transition must be experienced. This is a time of intense pain. There is no going back and no hurrying the outcome. Sometimes it seems like the end is too far in the distance, and there is not enough strength to endure to the end. Nothing else matters except getting through it. To make it successfully through transition, the laboring mother must breathe in a controlled manner to endure the pain and avoid losing control. She must rivet her focus on and concentrate fully on her labor coach. She must lean into the pain to overcome it and use it toward the birthing process. She must work with the process and not against it for a smooth, yet not painless, transition to bring forth life.

In this much-unexpected season of my life, I felt like I was in transition. God was, indeed, intending to birth something in me, but it was not the life story I had written in my own imagination. It was very painful, all-consuming, and unrelenting. My only course of action was to keep breathing in His Word, fully relying on His Spirit within me to illuminate what I so desperately needed to hear. I needed to fix my eyes on Jesus, my only hope of survival lest I tumble off the steep precipice on the way up this mountain. I had to lean into the pain and bring it honestly and completely to God in prayer, nothing hidden, nothing denied or justified. There was no room to cover up the truth of all I was experiencing. It was a time of full exposure and complete transparency. Tears were to flow freely to

---

[10] John 10:10

wash away the pent-up sadness and work through the grief that had now revisited me.

When Ernie died, there were so many things that needed to be done. Looking back, I see that the healing work of grief was often displaced by the tyranny of the urgent. There were so many fires that needed to be extinguished. There were so many others for whom to care and so many needs to be met. There were children to take care of, IEPs to be overseen, weddings to plan, graduations to celebrate, bills to be paid, cars to fix, houses to repair, employment to attend to so I could pay those bills. The list was endless and exhausting. My need to complete the immediate work of grief was deferred, as was my hope. This went on for many years. But now, in the fullness of His time, I was experiencing again the loss of Ernie and our dreams together as well as the loss of a dream that I had built up in my mind.

Though my tears had been scarce all my life, they were now flowing freely and at inconvenient times, in my estimation. What I was unable to put into words, my tears finally spoke freely. Without realizing it, I was finally letting Him into the hidden places of my heart that had been walled up by survival strategies. I thought I had found life and then it was dashed, again. As tears spoke my agony, they were also washing away the dirt that had covered the hidden treasure that was buried for so long to bring me His life.

There are a couple of different words that the Greek uses for life. One is "bios."[11] That is the physical life we have. I see it as the one dimensional, black and white, still-life, paper-doll way of existence. Another is "zoe."[12] This is the John 10:10 abundant life that Jesus came to bring. I see this as the three dimensional, living color, high definition, fully animated way of life. But how do you get from "bios" to "zoe"?

God tells us that, as we delight in Him, He will give us the desires of our heart.[13] That doesn't mean that He will give us everything we desire like spoiled children. There are many things I

---

[11] Strong's concordance #979, BIOS
[12] Strong's concordance #2222, ZOE
[13] Psalm 37:4

thought I desired that I'm glad, in retrospect, that He didn't give me. No, God promises to place *His* desires in our hearts as we delight in Him and not in our fleshly desires.

To delight in Him means to be soft and pliable.[14] My greatest hope for peace was to get out of my own head. I needed to "be transformed by the renewing of my mind, that I could prove what is that good and acceptable and perfect will of God."[15] I needed to trust Him enough to be pliable, to let Him mold me into who He created me to be and allow Him to give me the life He desired for me. I needed to allow Him to "abide" with me and be totally honest with Him. I needed to let Him see the real me, though He already knew. He wanted me to see it for myself. I needed to allow His Word to change my thinking to His thinking. That's where I would find His peace and abundant life.

Not only does God provide a make-over for our unsettled minds, He gives us shoes of peace as part of His armor. "And having shod your feet with the preparation of the gospel of peace."[16] He has us covered from head to toe.

I love walking barefoot in the cool sand at the beach. There is nothing more freeing and refreshing. But what happens when the sand gets too hot and there are broken shells and rocks hidden in the sand? In my discontent, it felt like my cool walk at the beach had become painful. My peace had been totally disturbed. I needed to retrace my steps in the gospel of peace. I had to mine some treasures in His Word that could sustain my walk with Him, assure my way on this slippery slope and keep me from following my own path and desires.

During World War II, army forces placed stakes in the ground to wound the feet of the opposing soldiers. They knew that if the feet were compromised, the soldier would be taken out of battle. Our enemy knows that this is true in spiritual battle too. If our feet are not ready to travel, it can be very difficult to stay on the path before

---

[14] Strong's concordance #6026, ANOG
[15] Romans 12:2
[16] Ephesians 6:15

us and to stand firm in His peace when our faith is challenged. We can lose the battle. I wanted to throw in the towel with this battle of my desires. It was relentless. But God threw it back at me and said, "Wipe your face, soldier, we're going somewhere!"

I began to study the Christmas story again. Prior to the celebration of Christmas, we observe advent. Advent is the hopeful expectation of the arrival of Messiah. How do we apply that hopeful expectation to the seasons of "hope deferred" that we experience? How do we get from the *hope* (active, confident expectation) of advent to the *peace* of advent? The shalom peace of advent is described by Paul as this:

> And God's peace [shall be yours, that tranquil state of a soul assured of its salvation through Christ, and so fearing nothing from God and being content with its earthly lot of whatever sort that is, that peace] which transcends all understanding shall garrison and mount guard over your hearts and minds in Christ Jesus. (Philippians 4:7 AMP)

I was far from "being content with my earthly lot." I had started to write my own story in my head and ask God to bless it. How did I get so disoriented? Luke tells us that we are "blessed" by trusting belief and confidence that God will bring to the fullest extent of all *He* has promised.[17] Mary expressed it as magnifying her God over her circumstance.[18] As children, we may have been agitated and impatient in expectation of Christmas. This is replaced by peace as we mature. (That is unless you are a parent preparing for Christmas. Then our own self-imposed expectations can still trip us up.) But as we lean on our understanding of Him and not on ourselves, we can know, assuredly, that the greatest gift has been given in Christ. He

---

[17] Luke 1:45 (emphasis added)
[18] Luke 1:46

has given us His peace.[19] It is not the peace that the world gives in the form of artificial pacification and instant gratification. It is peace that will sustain us in the fiercest storm. The storm may not let up, but He will surely steady us in it. That was my experience. I needed to cling to Him. He holds out His peace for us. Will we receive it, unwrap it and put it to use? That was the choice before me.

Even though I found myself back in the valley of the shadow of death, I had to keep walking through and not camp out in this dark and discontented place. I could not set up my own camp of artificial happiness in a place where I did not belong. The gaping hole of grief that had again overtaken me and the desire for relief left me vulnerable to counterfeit peace. I had to lean on all I knew of Him, minute by minute. I learned that there cannot be shadows unless the sun is present. Just ask the groundhog on a cloudy day. The groundhog may promise us an early spring in the absence of his shadow but Jesus, the Son, offers us His abiding presence as we look beyond the shadows in that deep, dark valley.

He has assured me in His Word that He is with me in this valley.[20] He is Immanuel.[21] He made a way for the gaping hole in my heart to be filled with His perfect peace,[22] His wholeness, His Shalom.[23] Everything else would be a temporary fix. We celebrate Who Jesus was—a Baby in a manger. We celebrate Who He is; God with us and in us because of the cross. We celebrate Who He will be; God over His kingdom in heaven where the battle will finally be over. In the meantime, it can be a steep climb, but we are not alone. I needed to press in to Him even closer. I needed to sing that song of ascent as I made the journey to the higher place of praise and worship, Zion.

Jesus came so He could be seen and experienced. He came close to us so He could redeem us and buy us back from the slavery of sin and selfishness. He came to show the way back home to the Father,

---

[19] John 14:27
[20] Psalm 23:4
[21] Isaiah 7:14
[22] Isaiah 26:3
[23] Streng's concordance #7965, SHALOM

where we rightfully belong. He died so we could stand unashamed before the Father, hidden in Him. In my darkness, He was knocking on the door of my heart asking to take up more of my residence, to abide with me even more. He is ever present in His fullness. It's not His availability that is lacking. It is my allowance of access. Every day, I need to choose to let Him in even more, to make more room for Him so that His light can illuminate my darkness until He brings me home.

He is still birthing something in me. Perhaps it is this testimony that you hold in your hands. It certainly has brought me much joy and excitement to write it, with a renewed hope of bringing hope to others. Perhaps it was a birth of my desire to speak the Gospel on social media. Hey, blame Facebook. The question it asks me every time I open it is, "What's on your mind, Cindy?" Well, I'm glad you asked! But the greatest treasure I have found is His peace in the transition. I don't know what's up ahead, but I know Who is already there. I know that He owns the cattle on a thousand hills,[24] and the earth is His footstool.[25] I know He is my Father and He will give good gifts to those who ask Him.[26] So I keep asking. I know that I don't have to write my own story because His story for me is so much better!

Lord, thank You for continually walking with me through the "lo" and dark places. Thank You for keeping me close to You even when I wrestle with You or want to run away. Thank You for redirecting my misunderstood hope. Okay, and thank You for those dang tears that continue to seep through my walls of self-preservation. Continue to conform me back into the image in which I was created, into Your image. My best hope is in You and that will never be deferred. It has already been secured for me as an anchor for my soul[27] on the cross.

"Lo, I am with you always, even to the end of the age" (Matthew 28:20).

---

[24] Psalm 50:10
[25] Isaiah 66:1
[26] Matthew 7:11
[27] Hebrews 6:19

CHAPTER 20

How Big?

The Lord Who delivered me from the paw of the lion and the paw of the bear will deliver me from the hand of this Philistine.

—1 Samuel 17:37

How big is my God? I have heard that question over and over again as I faced the unavoidable uncertainty and changeability of my future as a widow. Scripture is overflowing with accounts of God doing great and wonderful things. There is no doubt regarding what is recorded. My doubt rises up when I wonder what God will do for me. What is certain for me?

Foolishness or greed would cause me to believe God for a fully staffed mansion, a big expensive car or the trip of a lifetime. God *wants* me to prosper, right? The apostle John, the disciple whom Jesus loved, prayed that we would prosper in all things and be in good health.[28] What would make me prosper more than having the stress and striving in my life eased? Hmmm, if I really spend some time with God, I'm sure He will gladly answer *that* question for me. His idea of prosperity and His purpose for it are not the same as mine. His thoughts are not my thoughts and His ways are not my ways.[29]

---

[28] 3 John 2
[29] Isaiah 55:8

The meaning of the word prosper, in the Greek is "*euodóō* (*eú*, 'well, good' and *Ihodós*, 'a journey on a particular road')—properly, to go on a prosperous journey; (figuratively) to be *on the right* (*profitable*) *path*, i.e. leading to real success (good fortune) where someone truly '*prospers, is prospered*.'" [30]

John prays that we would be on the right road with God that we will be on the same page with Jesus in our desires. It is not that God will not lavish us with delightful things, but He has an eternal purpose for everything He does. His acts are not random but are intended to make His glory known. All that happens to me is intended to conform me into the image of Christ,[31] into the image in which I was created.[32] In my own ways and thoughts, if He were to "bless" me with certain things, it would certainly turn into "glory to me." He knows my heart and is faithful enough to spare me that pain. But for what does God want me to believe Him?

In the past, I have been caught up in the herd mentality of the prosperity Gospel. It caused me to believe God for the biggest and best. That distortion happens when we gather with others who are seeking the hand of God and not necessarily His face. It will lead us to believe that God will do things and provide things for us that are not really a part of His plan or purpose at this time. That mindset will cause me to believe for something that I *want* to happen instead of trusting God to provide according to His promises. It can cause me to follow the crowd into the Red Sea at a time when God has not said to go that way. At best, I will only come out wet and out of breath. At worst, I will emerge with my faith drowned and needing significant resuscitation. Sticking to the truth of His Word can be challenging when our desire outweighs our trust. That is a dangerous place.

So for what does God want me to believe Him? I have been involved with churches facing large financial decisions. These decisions, if executed in a godly way, certainly required God's blessing

---

[30] Strong's concordance #2137, EUODOO
[31] Romans 8:29
[32] Genesis 1:27

and His direction. We surely didn't want to plummet into *that* Red Sea unless God had given the go ahead. If we selfishly believe that nothing is impossible for God,[33] we can easily jump on the band-wagon of believing God for anything that seems humanly impossible and find ourselves in over our head. I have been on that bandwagon before. It is a slippery slope that has lost many passengers in its wake. It is forging on ahead without God's direction or blessing. It is pursuing what I want, not what He wants.

So where is the balance between the line of "me of little faith"[34] and plummeting into the Red Sea without direction? Perhaps it is found on the road of obedience. With regard to finances, I know beyond a shadow of a doubt that, as I am faithful to give God His tithe, He will open up the floodgates of heaven to bless me with more that I can contain.[35] He has proven Himself faithful to me in that time and time again. That kind of believing for His blessing requires faith and obedience. God says, "Test Me in this." That requires action. God says to put your money where your mouth is. "Let Me prove Myself faithful. Cause Me to bless you!"

In Exodus 16, God provided manna for His people faithfully every single day except for the seventh day. He told them to collect just enough for the day and not try to stock up ahead of time. If they were disobedient, the manna was found rotted the next day. He told them to collect twice as much on the sixth day to feed themselves on day seven, the Sabbath. If they were disobedient, there was no provision on day 7, so they went hungry. Their blessing was dependent on their obedience.

For what can I trust God? I don't have to look far into the future. I can trust Him for today. If I look too far ahead, I become overwhelmed. But if I keep my focus on what He has already done and what He will do today, I can walk in trust and belief. As David faced his giant, He trusted the God Who had already proven Himself to

---

[33] Luke 1:37
[34] Matthew 8:26
[35] Malachi 3:10

David. He didn't have to trust some pie-in-the-sky hope. He trusted in the proven ability and solid promises of His God.

Did God provide all that I needed yesterday? Yes. Did He make Himself known to me yesterday? Yes. Did He cause me to wake up today? The answer to all those questions is a resounding "yes." It is when I allow myself to get too caught up in the more-than-tomorrow future that I get lost in uncertainty. But my future is secure, one day at a time, one minute and one dollar at a time because God has already proven Himself faithful today.

God is the "I AM."[36] He is not the "I was" or the "I will be," though He was, and He will be. He is the same yesterday, today and forever.[37] There is so much to my infinite God that I cannot fathom His depths in my human understanding. I need to trust Him for today.

David didn't fear the paw of the lion or the paw of the bear. He didn't fear what was ahead of him because he had seen what was behind him. He didn't fear Goliath because he knew his giant God. And I don't need to fear poverty or lack or loneliness or abandonment. I don't need to fear because God has always delivered me. Through it, He has shown me more and more of Himself and His character. I have always come out knowing Him more confidently and trusting Him more completely. He has always brought me out better and more complete in Him, looking just a little more like Jesus.

David knew what it meant to be in need, and He penned it in Psalm 23. As a shepherd, he knew how dependent his sheep were on his shepherding ability. David knew that sometimes he had to lead his sheep through the valley of the shadow of death. These were dark and scary places found on the way to green pastures and still water. But David declared that his Lord was his shepherd. He lacked nothing! As the sheep of God's pasture,[38] we can claim the same. Many times, I have declared that in faith. "I lack nothing!." That is, until

---

[36] Exodus 3:14
[37] Hebrews 13:8
[38] Psalm 100:3

my desires get misaligned with His will. When I find myself discontent, I need to ask God where I have stepped out of alignment with Him. Where have I stepped off from His path of prosperity?

Paul said, "I have *learned* the secret of being content in whatever state I'm in."[39] The original word for *learned*[40] is much like the word for disciple. As I follow Jesus, I learn from Him. If I follow my flesh or my culture, I learn a different way of prosperity and contentment. This has been a life-long training for me. As I stay on His path, I will find real contentment, regardless of my circumstances. I will honestly be able to declare that I lack nothing. It is countercultural and many times against my flesh. But again, God is faithful to return me to a place of contentment as I trust in Him.

I can trust Him to lead me in His paths of righteousness, not in my own way because it's for His name's sake.[41] He will do good to me to prove His goodness, according to His name which is His character. And that good always makes me look more and more like Jesus.[42] He says goodness and mercy will follow me all the days of my life.[43] It's not a self-centered goodness. It's not what I consider good to bring me ease and pleasure. The Hebrew word for goodness means beneficial.[44] He will do whatever is beneficial in my transformation. His mercy will not wink at my disobedience. His mercy, in the Hebrew is the word *chesed*, which means lovingkindness.[45] This is the kind of love that makes me better and does not indulge me. I amassed this definition of *chesed* from different sources that always brings me back into alignment with Him: It is lovingkindness, covenant loyalty, the consistent, unchanging, ever faithful, relentless, constantly pursuing, lavish, extravagant, unrestrained, furious, patiently persistent, jealous, undeserved, dependable blessing of covenant love of our Father God. That's what's following me all the days of my life.

---

[39] Philippians 4:11
[40] Strong's concordance #3129, MANTHANO
[41] Psalm 23:3
[42] Romans 8:29
[43] Psalm 23:6
[44] Strong's concordance #2896b, TOB
[45] Strong's concordance #2617a, CHESED

And it's not just following behind. It is pursuing me. The Hebrew for "follow" in Psalm 23:6 literally means pursuing., chasing after.[46]

So I am a sheep in His pasture and His goodness and mercy are the sheep dogs corralling me into His place of perfect provision and protection! How big is my God? He is big enough to get me through today and do great things with it for His glory. He is big enough to supply all my needs according to His riches in glory in Christ.[47] He doesn't supply all my needs from my meager portion. He supplies them abundantly from the storehouse of His riches. He wants me on His path of prosperity, protection and provision. He will chase me into His abundance with His goodness and mercy. Some days it takes a *really big* God to accomplish that for me but He is faithful.

Lord, Thank You that You are big enough to keep me safe. Thank You that You are teaching me to be content in every situation. I don't need to fear because I know that Your protection and provision reflect Your character, Your name. When I am feeling chased or hunted down, I can remember that it is You Who is pursuing me with Your goodness and mercy. I know that You are always good and always desire good for me. I have no need to fear or doubt You.

"He has delivered us from the power of darkness and conveyed us into the kingdom of the Son of His love, in whom we have redemption through His blood, the forgiveness of sins" (Colossians 1:13–14).

---

[46] Strong's concordance #7291, RADAPH
[47] Philippians 4:19

PART 5

Treasures in Searching

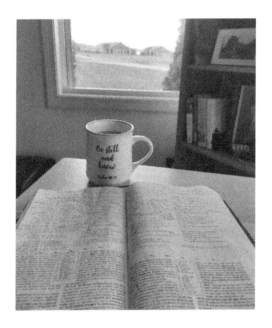

And you will seek Me and find Me, when you
search for Me with all your heart.

—Jeremiah 29:13

CHAPTER 21

Busted

Preparing for a study, I started to read the second chapter of 1 Peter. I had intended to read and study the whole chapter, but I got stuck on the very first verse.

"Therefore, laying aside all malice, all deceit, hypocrisy, envy, and all evil speaking (slander)."[1]

It didn't sound that bad at first. I am a Christian. How could there be any malice in me. By the way, what is malice, anyway? I am a truthful person, not putting up a hypocritical front. And I don't envy what others have. I am satisfied with my job, my home, my ability to pay the bills. And slander—far be it for me—or is it that far? Maybe I should take a closer look, especially since God uses some pretty inclusive words in this portion of Scripture. Two "alls" and an "every" don't leave much room for exception!

Let's start with the first word: *therefore*. That usually means that there is something very important immediately preceding the statement. It begs the question, what is it there for? Reading the end of the previous chapter, God says this: "but the Word of the Lord stands forever."[2]

I always want to fully understand what God expects of me and what He has to offer to help me meet those expectations. As you have

---

[1] 1 Peter 2:1
[2] 1 Peter 1:25

seen, I often find it helpful to look back to the original language. It gives me a much deeper and clearer understanding of God's Word, sometimes deeper and clearer than that for which I am prepared.

The Greek translation for "Word" in this Scripture is *rhema*, meaning "a word as uttered by a Living Voice."[3] I can almost hear it from God's lips to my ears. It is the Word that lights up and jumps off the page, written specifically for me.

"Lord" is translated as *kurios*.[4] It refers to the One who has absolute power, authority, and sovereignty. That leaves me out. He is the one with absolute authority.

"Stands" is translated as *meno*,[5] abide or endure…forever.

Putting it all together, it says that everything that God says is directed personally to me, it is the final, uncontested authority, and it will never change, ever. It will not change with age or customs or culture or fads. It will always say the same thing, forever.

I am reminded of another Scripture regarding the Word of God.

> For the word of God is alive and active. Sharper than any double-edged sword, it penetrates even to dividing soul and spirit, joints and marrow; it judges the thoughts and attitudes of the heart. Nothing in all creation is hidden from God's sight. Everything is uncovered and laid bare before the eyes of Him to Whom we must give account.[6]

Having the thoughts and attitudes of my heart exposed and laid bare before the Creator and Absolute Authority of the universe causes me to reconsider. I definitely need a more thorough evaluation of myself based on the commands in 1 Peter 2:1.

"Rid yourself of ALL malice." "All" would include the obvious acts as well as those hidden in the deepest recesses of my heart

---

[3] Strong's concordance #4487, RHEMA
[4] Strong's concordance #2962, KURIOS
[5] Strong's concordance #3306, MENO
[6] Hebrews 4:12–13

and masked by the cover of good intent. Malice, according to Mr. Webster, is the desire to do harm to someone. It is wishing that something bad would happen to them or deliberately desiring to annoy them. It is the opposite of the desire to build someone up and promote them.

I begin to feel the twinge of conviction. Do I ever secretly wish that someone would not be promoted or given a part or a certain job? Do I ever wish that someone didn't have something that I desired but didn't have? Do I always desire the best for others, no matter what affect it may have on me? Okay, Lord. I may have glossed over that one a bit too quickly. I have known malice.

"All deceit." I am not really guilty of outright lying but could I be accused of not presenting the whole truth? Am I at all dishonest in my daily interactions with people? But, Lord, You know where I work, where I play, where I live. Surely You understand. His response, "Understand, yes. Excuse, no." Okay, guilty again.

Hypocrisy? Surely not. I would never be considered a "whitewashed tomb."[7] Or am I guilty of insincerity and pretense, of acting a part, not showing who I really am? How about the number of times people sincerely ask me how I am, and I slap on a plastic smile and say "fine." Or they ask if I need any help and I deny it. Okay, God, I could use a good inside cleaning.

Envy? Material possessions have never been really important to me. I don't struggle with keeping up with the Joneses or coveting other's things. But wait. Looking at where I have been may make me reevaluate envy. How many times have I really envied families who have a mom and a dad to share responsibilities, support each other, and just comfort each other when the going gets rough? How many times have I seen couples walking hand in hand or dining out together and let discontent move in? Again, I know that God understands, but He will not excuse that response on my part. It's not the response that He desires because He wants the best for me and that's not it!

---

[7] Matthew 23:27

Evil speaking? Slander? I would never intentionally spread a lie about someone. But how many times have I repeated "information" about someone without being certain of its accuracy, perhaps even in the name of prayer?!

Okay. I'm five for five and batting zero. I have taken a closer look and discovered that I am not as innocent as I had initially assessed. My thoughts and the attitudes and intentions of my heart have been laid bare and exposed. I am helpless, in my own effort, to change any of it. The darkness of my own sin and depravity seems to unearth everything but treasures. But wait.

Continuing on in Hebrews 4:14, I find another "therefore." Since I can't hide anything from God and everything is known to Him, He has provided me with a Great High Priest, Jesus Christ, my Savior.

> Seeing (therefore) then that we have a great High Priest who has passed through the heavens, Jesus the Son of God, let us hold fast our confession. For we do not have a High Priest who cannot sympathize with our weaknesses, but was in all points tempted as we are, yet without sin. Let us therefore come boldly to the throne of grace, that we may obtain mercy and find grace to help in time of need.[8]

Standing confidently before God's throne doesn't mean arrogantly. The Greek word for *confidence* is *parresia*.[9] It is a combination of two Greek words meaning to speak all, free to speak honestly and transparently. I have this freedom because the blood of Jesus removes my guilt. His work on the cross allows me to stand humbly yet confidently before the throne. I can pour out my deepest regrets before Him and find His mercy and grace when I least deserve it. Jesus stands in front of me before the Father. He pleads my case, not

---

[8] Hebrews 4:14–16
[9] Strong's concordance #3955, PARRESIA

accepting my unacceptable behavior but giving me endless chances to get it right. God the Father sees Jesus standing in His authority on my behalf and pardons me. Now, that's amazing grace.

The entire Old and New Testament is proof that God gives us endless chances to get it right. That has been His goal since the fall of man by Adam and Eve in the Garden.

Just two short chapters into God's Book we find Adam and Eve guilty of doing what displeased God. That was okay. We all make mistakes. The biggest problem came when they ran and hid from the only One who could right their mistake. God gave them repeated chances to come clean, but they ended up continually denying their true guilt and responsibility by blaming each other and relying on excuses. As a result, they were banished from the Garden. They lost their privilege of constant, unbroken communion with God the Father, Who supplied their every need.

The rest of Scripture, all the way through Revelation, is God's entire plan to restore us to that constant communion with Him, naked and exposed, yet unashamed. It will not change until His new heaven and new earth descends and Christ reigns over both. We are, presently, in the Age of Grace but it will not last forever. The Age of Judgment will come when we will all have to give an account for ourselves. It's like when our monthly bills come. We have a grace period. That is the time between the end of the billing cycle and the date payment is due. In Christ, our debt has been paid. Apart from Christ, there will no longer be payment for our sin, and we will owe the debt of the wrath of God.

My heart is deceitful above all things.[10] It causes me to see myself inaccurately. It causes me to deny what might really be inside. It causes me to blame others, make excuses and try to defend myself before God when it would be so much easier and more fruitful to confess, agree with Him and get on with it.

God does not use His Word to condemn me. He does not intend it to put me down or to make me think of myself as a no-good person. His Word is the fertilizer with which my greatest happiness

---

[10] Jeremiah 17:9

and fulfillment can be produced. If I use His Word as He intended, it produces fruit, more fruit and much fruit for His glory[11] and for my good. If I follow His instructions, I will be the happiest, the most satisfied and the most fulfilled. Therein lies the treasure to that darkness.

As my blind spots, the things that I can't see about myself, are exposed by the Word of God, I hold them out for Him to heal. I am powerless to clean up my own act. Oh, maybe I can make it look good on the outside, but the inside is still a mess. You can only keep that mess at bay for so long before it starts pouring out through words and actions. One little bump or jostle and there is that mess spewing out all over the place. That is my interpretation of "For out of the overflow of the heart the mouth speaks."[12] So how do I get the inside cleaned up? God says, "If we confess our sins, He is faithful and just to forgive us our sins and cleanse (purify) us from all unrighteousness."[13]

The Greek word for *confess* is *homologeo*.[14] It is a combination of two common words: *homo*, meaning the same, and *logo*, meaning word. It means saying the same words or agreeing with what God says. Confession is not saying I'm sorry because if the truth were known, sometimes I'm not really sorry. I'm just sorry I got caught. Confession is literally telling God that I did what He already saw me do. Holding it up to the mirror of His Word, I can see how my actions grieve God. And they only grieve Him because it's not His best for me. To confess is to agree with God that what I thought, did or the way I acted was not right according to His expectations, His unchanging Word. It doesn't factor in my flesh, my culture, my opinions or justifications. It is not the changing standards and vocabulary of my culture.

No, confession is not initially a felt sorrow. It is saying to God, "Yes, I did it. I know You saw it and I know You don't like it." I ask for the forgiveness that Jesus has already provided. I agree with God

---

[11] John 15:8
[12] Matthew 12:34
[13] I John 1:9
[14] Strong's concordance #3670, HOMOLOGEO

that Jesus has already paid my penalty and has credited my account. All the forgiveness I have needed and will ever need is seen on the cross. I just need to agree with Him that I am out of alignment with what He expects without hiding, blaming others or using a multitude of excuses.

As I agree with him, He is faithful, *pistos*.[15] He is worthy of belief, trust, and confidence because He has proven Himself worthy time and time again. And He is just, *dikaios*.[16] He expects the same of everyone, and He is willing and able to empower me and anyone else who will ask, to walk in alignment with what He expects.

And He will forgive, *aphiemi*.[17] He will send my mistakes away from His remembrance. He will let go of His power and His right to punish me for my wrongdoing. And He will not bring it up the next time I stand before Him with the same confession.

"As far as the east is from the west, so far has He removed our transgressions from us."[18]

I have heard that the east never meets the west. I guess you can't get any greater distance than that. He will not hold it against me. He does not keep score and He expects the same of me toward others. Yes. You read that right!

Not only will He forgive us, He will also purify, *katharizo*,[19] us. The picture of catharsis is very clear to me. I spent a portion of my pediatric nursing career in pediatric gastroenterology. This required me to assist in colonoscopies. If the catharsis or cleansing is not complete, the results are readily visible and not very desirable. I can really appreciate a good purification given that experience! God doesn't waste any experiences, does He? Christ loves us and gave Himself up for us that we could be washed in the water of His Word that we might be holy, having no spots or stains.[20] A good cleansing is what He has promised to do for me if I apply His truth as directed. And

15 Strong's concordance #4103, PISTOS
16 Strong's concordance #1342, DIKAIOS
17 Strong's concordance #863, APHIEMI
18 Psalm 103:12
19 Strong's concordance #2511, KATHARIZO
20 Ephesians 5:26–27

He is faithful and just to purify us from *all* unrighteousness. Here we are back at the beginning again. He is willing and able to put me back in alignment and agreement with Him in all areas so that I can enjoy constant fellowship with Him.

"Therefore, laying aside all malice, all deceit, hypocrisy, envy, and all evil speaking, as newborn babes, desire the pure milk of the word, that you may grow thereby, if indeed you have tasted that the Lord is gracious."[21]

Peter did not speak theoretically. He spoke out of practical application of what he had learned while walking personally with Jesus. Peter knew malice. He drew his sword and cut off someone's ear.[22] It was in Jesus's defense, but it was outside of what Jesus desired. Peter knew deceit. Peter was warned by Jesus that satan had asked to sift him as wheat.[23] Peter, in his own strength, promised to always stick by Jesus. He had deceived himself and did not acknowledge his own weaknesses. Peter knew hypocrisy. When asked if he knew Jesus, Peter denied it…three times.[24] Peter knew envy. He was likely among the disciples when they were disputing about who would be greatest.[25] Peter knew about evil talk. He was rebuked by Jesus when he denied that Jesus would be crucified, not being mindful of the Father's plan.[26] These are just a few of Peter's mistakes that were recorded in Scripture. They are given, not as a microscope to evaluate Peter but as a mirror for us to see our own reflection.

We can look at all of Peter's missteps and find great hope and encouragement. Two of my favorite words in Scripture are "and Peter."[27] The women were at Jesus's tomb on Sunday morning. They found the stone rolled away and the body of Jesus no longer there. An angel explained that Jesus was risen and was going before them into Galilee. Jesus had told Peter this plan earlier when He predicted

---

[21] 1 Peter 2:1–3
[22] John 18:10
[23] Luke 22:31
[24] Luke 22:54–62
[25] Luke 9:46
[26] Matthew 16:23
[27] Mark 16:7

Peter's denial.[28] The angel told the women to go tell the disciples "and Peter." Jesus knew that Peter needed to hear that his mistakes were not fatal. He specifically called Peter out so that he would know that he was still in the game. Often, Peter is criticized for going back to fishing after the crucifixion.[29] This plan, however, brought him to Lake Tiberias, which is the Sea of Galilee. Peter was in the exact location foretold to meet Jesus for his public restoration.[30]

Jesus never rejected Peter. He was committed to teaching him and nurturing his growth as His disciple. In spite of all the many times he failed, Jesus confirmed to Peter that he was still welcome and expected to follow Him. Even after his public restoration, Peter is walking along with Jesus and is immediately reentangled in envy. Peter looked back at John[31] and wanted to compare himself with John. He asks Jesus, "What about him? The one closest to You, leaning on Your breast?" Jesus's response is life-changing and freeing for all of us: "What is that to you? You follow Me."[32]

God does not compare me to anyone except His Son. I don't need to worry about how far someone else is off base. I just need to be sure my foot is on the bag, so I don't get thrown out. Peter is proof of that. He became a powerful preacher of the Gospel as witnessed in the second chapter of Acts. Having been empowered by the Holy Spirit at Pentecost, Peter delivered the first sermon of the New Testament church. Three thousand souls were saved that day, and the church grew daily.[33] Peter stood on the truth of his name change from Peter to "rock."[34] Peter himself was not the rock. The truth of his confession that Jesus is the Christ, the Son of the Living God[35] is the rock. Peter was fallible. Jesus, the Rock, is infallible and He wants to purify me for Himself. My confession of His Lordship and His

---

[28] Mark 14:28
[29] John 21:1
[30] John 21:15–19
[31] John 21:21
[32] John 21:22
[33] Acts 2:41, 47
[34] John 1:42
[35] Matthew 16:16

strength as my rock is the ground on which He builds His church and His kingdom as I follow Him!

Yes, Peter knew the stumbling blocks first-hand. He also knew the forgiveness and gracious nature of His Savior first-hand and that made all the difference.

Yes, Lord, I am guilty of malice, deceit, hypocrisy, envy, and slander. I agree that my reactions are not pleasing to You. But You do not convict me of these things to make me feel guilty. You illuminate these blind spots for me so that You can realign them for my benefit. I am a much happier person when I am not weighed down and burdened with malice, deceit, hypocrisy, envy, and slander. I am freer to be who You created me to be without them. It doesn't matter why I felt the need to carry them in the first place. Thank You for Your promise to forgive me and to cleanse me from all unrighteousness. Let the catharsis begin and the fellowship resume! I choose to follow You!

> Create in me a clean heart, O God,
> And renew a steadfast spirit within me.
> Do not cast me away from Your presence,
> And do not take Your Holy Spirit from me.
> Restore to me the joy of Your salvation,
> And uphold me by Your generous Spirit. (Psalm
>   51:10–12)

CHAPTER 22

The Canvas

I'm not much of an artist. In fact, I can't draw my own breath! I have great respect for someone who can take a blank surface and turn it into a thing of beauty. I have tried, and I have had friends who have tried to help me bring out my inner artist but she's really not in there. My attempts at being an artist can easily be compared to my spiritual life. I am God's masterpiece.[1] In the Greek, the word is *poiema*,[2] His poem. He is the Potter; I am the clay, the work of His Hand,[3] His work of art.

He has created me in His image.[4] My life is intended to reflect what He wants to say. Jesus came to do the same but because Jesus was God, fully God and fully man, He could be the exact representation, the express image of the Father.[5] Unredeemed, I cannot reflect the accurate picture. Even redeemed, I am limited by the areas that I choose to keep for myself, my unsanctified places. His painting of me is, in part, what He wants to accomplish piece by piece as I relinquish it to Him. And we need each other in the body of Christ to complete the whole picture.

---

[1]   Ephesians 2:10
[2]   Strong's concordance #4161 POIEMA
[3]   Isaiah 64:8
[4]   Genesis 1:27
[5]   Hebrews 1:3

We are all a work in progress. God is building us up in Christ,[6] to His fullness.[7] The masterpiece will not be complete until we each see Jesus face-to-face. In the meantime, He is painting the picture of my life, the days He planned for me from before I was born.[8] The picture of my life was in His mind before He put brush to canvas. But will I trust Him with the masterpiece?

How often have I looked at my canvas and compared it to my friends, comparing my life to theirs. "Why does my life contain these strokes and theirs does not? Why can't I have those colors instead of these?" How often have I complained about the masterpiece that He is creating in me. How often have I judged by the unfinished condition in myself and others. I have no idea what others have gone through to get those colors or what is ahead of them for which His strokes have prepared. I don't understand the depth of the master-piece. A true artist knows that there are many layers to a finished work of art. To judge it in the creating state is to miss the treasure that is intended.

Because creating is a multilayered and detailed process, I often give up before I can see the beauty come through. I convince myself that this is never going to work together for anything good, contrary to what He promises.[9] So I decide to take the brush in my own hands and create what I think the masterpiece should look like. The problem with that is that He knows what the masterpiece is supposed to look like. He knows that it is supposed to look like Jesus.[10] In my humanity, I think it should look like comfort, ease, happiness, unicorns, and rainbows. But the life of Jesus was none of that. His focus was on the joy set before Him,[11] which caused Him to endure the cross and the shame associated with it. He was not looking for the happiness that was dependent on His present circumstances. Happiness can quickly be stolen by changes in circumstances. It was

---

[6] Colossians 2:7
[7] Ephesians 4:13
[8] Psalm 139:16
[9] Roman 8:28
[10] Romans 8:29
[11] Hebrews 12:2

the joy of returning to His throne at the right hand of His Father and making a way for us to join Him that caused Him to endure. There was very little, if any, comfort and ease associated with His journey to bring me home. So when my life's canvas starts to look like a relief map, with all the mountains to climb and the dark valleys to cross, I can remember that He is in control of the brush.

There are times, however, that I have tried to grab the brush and change what He is trying to create. "Lord, wouldn't this look nice here? This would really add so much to the masterpiece that You have in mind. Lord, this mountain is a little high and these clouds are a little dark. How about a little sunshine over here?" I have tried to make my life make sense according to my own understanding. That causes a detour from His intended plan. But He is patient with me. As a parent, I have, at times, had to learn to let my children develop through their mistakes. Our loving Father is much more tolerant and patient. His Word speaks of His forbearance.[12]

The word *forbearance*, in the Greek, is *anoche*.[13] The pronunciation sound like "an okay." I find that very comforting. When I mess up His masterpiece, He doesn't just rip up the canvas on me. He gives me "an okay." He is patient to use my mis-strokes in spite of me. He knows my heart, and He knows my heart is His. Because my heart is His, Jesus will apply His blood to my mistake and make it as if I had never sinned. That is His justification, "just as if" I hadn't messed up. In fact, He will pour His blood out on the entire canvas of my life and make it as white as snow so I can start over! How He can use the crimson of His blood to create a fresh clean, white canvas is beyond my comprehension. But He is God, and I am not. For an unskilled artist like me, there couldn't be any better news!

He is my Justifier because I have faith in Him.[14] He pleads my case and defends me and my masterpiece as I let Him put the colors and strokes in the places He desires. If I choose to not have faith in Him and paint my own idea of a masterpiece, He will not force

---

[12] Romans 3:25
[13] Strong's concordance #463 ANOCHE
[14] Romans 3:26

my hand. He will not cover my canvas unless I ask Him to do so. He will allow me to display a mess instead of His masterpiece for as long as I desire. If I insist on going my own way, He will give me up to my stubborn desires. My continuous rejection of Him and rebellion against Him will result in my own destruction.[15] The choice is mine. For an old Vermonter like me, that can be terrifying. That old independent spirit can lead me astray in a heartbeat. Thankfully, I have chosen to give my heart to Him. I have invited Him to take the paintbrush even when I think I can paint a better picture. I may kick and scream, complain, and cry; but He knows my heart is His. Like a patient parent, He will wait for my tantrum to wear itself out. He will wait for me to come to my senses, and He will renew my faith in Him. It is He who works in me to have the desire and the ability to do what pleases Him[16] because I have invited Him in and because I choose to stay with Him, no matter what.

My canvas is old, with many mis-strokes made by myself and made by others on my canvas. He is the only one Who can turn it into a thing of beauty. *He* promises to turn my ashes into beauty.[17] No matter how old and marred my canvas gets, as long as I look to Him, He will recreate and restore what He has planned for me. It is a plan for good and not for hurt and harm.[18] No matter how many mistakes have been made, He can turn it around, cover it with His grace to display His glory, the truth of Who He is, instead of my inadequacies or injuries. And that, my friend, is a beautiful masterpiece!

Lord, I want to always submit to You because You are God, and I am not. Sometimes my actions defy my desire, but I am thankful that You know my heart. I am grateful that You will not leave me to my own devices and destruction because I have asked to be Yours. I have invited You to be Lord of my life and to cover me with Your sacrificial blood. I believe that You came to save me from myself. I believe that You overcame everything in this world up to and includ-

---

[15] Romans 1:24–25
[16] Philippians 2:13
[17] Isaiah 61:3
[18] Jeremiah 29:11

ing death. Thank You that You did not give me up to my own independence, but You showed me the error of my ways. You have been with me up the highest of mountains, through the darkest of valleys, in the thickest of fog and in the most intense heat. You have never left me, and You never will. You are mine, and I am Yours,[19] only because of Your grace. Lord, I pray that You will hold tightly to the paintbrush of my life. I pray that You will paint a masterpiece that will bring you much glory and pleasure and will display the unrivaled love and skill of my Artist!

> He who dwells in the secret place of the Most
>   High
> Shall abide under the shadow of the Almighty.
> I will say of the LORD, "He is my refuge and my
>   fortress;
> My God, in Him I will trust." (Psalm 91:1)

> Therefore, if anyone is in Christ, he is a new creation; old things have passed away; behold, all things have become new. (2 Corinthians 5:17)

---

[19] Song of Solomon 2:16

CHAPTER 23

Resolve

In the first chapters of Matthew, Jesus is confronting the religious leaders with the futility of their traditions and rituals. In chapter 15, Jesus is teaching about what is really clean and unclean in His estimation. It is here we are introduced to a Canaanite woman, seen as pagan and unclean in the Jewish culture. She is a woman (strike 1) and a Gentile (strike 2 in the eyes of the Pharisees). She cried out to Jesus, "Lord, Son of David, have mercy on me! My daughter is suffering terribly from demon-possession." She cried out and addressed Jesus as the Son of David. She knew Him as the promised Messiah, the promised Son of David, which is more than the religious leaders would claim. She, however, had no "rights" to claim from Him as she was not one who could claim to be one of the "lost sheep of Israel" to whom Jesus was sent[1] (strike 3). But she didn't take "out" for an answer. It may have been her deep desperation or her relentless hope or her solid faith in Who Jesus was. It may have been a combination of them all, but something caused her to press into Him. More than likely, it was because she was a mother crying out desperately for her child. Nothing could stop her. Against all odds, she cried out for Jesus's help.

---

[1] Matthew 15:24

Jesus, however, did not answer her plea. He ignored her. *What?* Yes, it says, "Jesus did not answer a word."[2] So the woman came and knelt before Him. It looks like her desperation was so overwhelming that she would risk being kicked aside rather than go away with empty hands and a broken heart. She cried out again, "Lord, help me."

She addressed Him as Lord. In the original language, that is *kurios*, meaning One with absolute authority and sovereignty.[3] She didn't have a backup plan or a plan B if Jesus rejected her plea. She had gone to the very top of all the authority she knew. There was no one else who could help her. She was at His full and complete mercy, abandoned to His grace alone. She had no rights. She had no entitlement. She pleaded to Him on the basis of His mercy, not her merit, as she had no merit to call on! The chasm between her poverty and the help she needed was endless and unbreachable in her own ability. She could take a chance and trust in what she may have heard about the faithfulness and compassion of this Jesus, or she could go home defeated. She chose to kneel before Him and cry out again for help. "Lord, help me."

Then, it seems that Jesus does, indeed, reject her plea, again! *Come on!* He answers, "It is not right to take the children's bread and toss it to their dogs." Wow, that sounds like she really *did* get kicked aside. She, however, is still not "out." This is where her authentic character really shines through. She did not turn away in offense to save face and let pride steal her victory. She didn't walk away and say, "I don't have to take this!" Contrast this to the attitude of the Pharisees reported by the disciples to Jesus when He addressed their hypocrisy. They were offended.[4] In the Greek, that means a stumbling block, a trap, something set to hinder right conduct.[5] It means to scandalize or outrage. Ultimately, offense is a trap set by the enemy to divert God's correction and growth. Though Jesus came

---

2   Matthew 15:23
3   Strong's concordance #2962 KURIOS
4   Matthew 15:12
5   Strong's concordance #4624 SKANDALIZO

to realign the Pharisee's misunderstandings, they were diverted from the truth by their offended attitude.

We see a similar story in Exodus 16. The Israelites were in the wilderness, part way between slavery in Egypt, on their way to the Promised Land. The trek was hard, and they became discouraged. They started grumbling and murmuring against their leaders. They looked back much like Lot's wife did at Sodom and Gomorrah.[6] Their memory was distorted by the harshness of the journey and their fatigue. Their remembrance was that they had it better in slavery in Egypt. They wanted to go back, forgetting the real pain of slavery. They wanted to go back to the familiar, unwilling to press on to the promise. Their discouragement led to feelings of helplessness, leaving them vulnerable to the "skandalizo" trap of the enemy. They were offended by the trial and open to the attacks of the enemy which sought to inhibit their growth.

But our desperate Canaanite mom was not going to be taken down. She had nothing to lose and everything to gain. She stuck with her Savior and instead of being offended, she pressed in even further, on to whatever promise Jesus had for her.

"Yes, Lord, but even the dogs eat the crumbs that fall from the Master's table." The immensity of her need could be met by the least of Christ. That was enough, just a crumb! Did she know that Jesus had fed the thousands with a few loaves and fishes? Did she know that He is the Bread of Life? Surely, He could have just a crumb left for her. In essence, she was saying, "I know that I have nothing deserving of You. I am the least of the least, a woman and a Gentile, a 'dog' in Your eyes." Yet her perceived identity did not stop her. She was desperate. She had a keen, gnawing, and deeply felt need. She realized that she was powerless to do anything in her own strength and ability. She was also nose to toes with the only One Who is all-powerful and fully able to rescue her and her child from this hell on earth. Did she ask herself, "Is He willing?" I'm not sure but she was certainly willing to stick around to find out.

---

[6] Genesis 19:26

Have you ever been in a situation where you were desperately in need of help and it seemed like you were invisible, put off, or put down? We have choices. We can walk away in offense, letting our pride and the enemy win or we can continue to press in, knowing the goodness and faithfulness of our God. The outcome is infinitely different. If all I can do is squeak out the name of Jesus as I choke on the dust of discouragement and impending defeat, He will come running.

Jesus answered, "Woman, you have great faith. Your request is granted." Her daughter was healed from that very hour.[7] What amazing joy! Yes, her daughter was rescued from demon possession, but more miraculously, Jesus called her "woman." In the original language, that is "gune,"[8] meaning wife, beloved, a term of endearment, "My lady." She went from being a dog to a bride. Wow, what a journey. But it didn't come easily or without tenacity. It didn't come by being easily offended or discouraged. Her tenacity was rewarded abundantly.

Jesus, Himself, knew how to be resolute. He knew how to be committed at all costs in the face of humiliation, mockery, and abuse on His way to the cross. And Jesus saw His character in this Canaanite woman. God says, "Because the Sovereign Lord helps me, I will not be disgraced. Therefore, I have set my face *like a flint*, and I know I will not be put to shame."[9]

"As the time approached for Him to be taken up to heaven, Jesus *resolutely* set out for Jerusalem."[10]

Flint is an extremely hard and unyielding stone. God likened the unbeliever's heart to flint. "They made their hearts as hard as flint, and would not listen to the law or to the words that the Lord Almighty had sent by His Spirit."[11] Our "gune" had some flint going on but it was *not* in her heart against her Savior. Jesus knew the strength and the steadfastness of her heart, and His mission was

---

[7] Matthew 15:28
[8] Strong's concordance #1135 GUNE
[9] Isaiah 50:7
[10] Luke 9:51
[11] Zechariah 7:11

to bring it out. Jesus wanted to reveal her strength to her. He wanted to show His disciples, who wanted to send her away, what tenacity really looked like. He wanted to show the religious leaders, who saw her as invaluable, how much He valued her. Jesus did this as an example to us.

Did "gune" know how strong she was? Did she know she could withstand more than one "no" or "wait" from her Savior? Likely not. But she was willing to first be humbled and then be honored by the One who would call her "gune." She was fully aware of her own unworthiness and that knowledge was pleasing to Jesus. It was His great pleasure to bless her. She was patient and persistent enough to have her vast chasm filled to overflowing with His unfailing and unfathomable love and faithfulness. She came with the need of her suffering child and left with a freed child *and* a new identity. God always gives us exceedingly, abundantly, above all we could ask or imagine. He always knows what we *really* need.

To understand the endearment of the name "gune," we can also look at Jesus's dying words on the cross. In His final hours with His dying breath, He looked at His mother at the foot of the cross. His heart broke for the grief she was experiencing. Jesus knew the pain of a mother for her child. He addressed His mother as "woman," "gune,"[12] a title of honor and respect for the woman He loved as a mother. Full of compassion, Jesus entrusted her care to the disciple whom He loved, John. Jesus, in His abundance, secured the future of His mother and a Canaanite woman.

Jesus says to me in this story of the Canaanite woman:

> Bring Me your unworthiness. Bring Me your need, your lack. Don't try to mask it, hide it or dress it up. Lay it at My feet. Know your need, not your entitlement. Come humbly. Plead mercy, not merit. Those I intend to honor the most, I humble. As you realize your own unworthiness and the chasm of your need, do not turn

---

[12] John 19:26

away in pride. Be abandoned to My grace and be abundantly and exceedingly blessed.

Lord, make me Your "gune"—pleasing, acceptable, and useful to You, for Your glory. Amen.

"I am my Beloved's, "And my Beloved is mine" (Song of Solomon 6:3).

CHAPTER 24

Truth: The Shame Buster

Well into my walk with the Lord, I spent a few years in Celebrate Recovery at my local church. It is a twelve-step, faith-based recovery program for all kinds of hurts, hang-ups, and habits. It is there and in the Word of God I discovered my true identity. The thorns with which I was born and the thorns of my environment were changed, allowing me to become more and more the woman I was created to be. I can declare confidently that I am a beloved child of God. I have been extended His grace, and I am continually being delivered from shame. It has taken me many years with much searching, but God's Word continues to illuminate His truth and defeat my shame, layer by layer. From the very beginning, the enemy has tried to gain a toe-hold in my life to build his kingdom of defeat and destruction. *But* God is building His kingdom of victory in its place. It is the treasure of the search.

I look back, not with a desire to go back but with a desire to gain wisdom and to be trained.[1] As I look back, I can see His goodness and mercy that Psalm 23 declares is pursuing and chasing after me.[2] It doesn't just follow me, as our English translation says. It hunts me down and goes in pursuit of me, according to the Greek![3] It proves to

---

[1]   Hebrews 12:11
[2]   Psalm 23:6
[3]   Strong's concordance #7291 RADAPH

me this truth: "But as for you, you meant evil against me; but God meant it for good, in order to bring it about as it is this day, to save many people alive."[4]

Looking back restores my (Genesis) 50:20 vision! I can see clearly that some things may have been intended for evil, but God used it for good and to conform me more and more into the image of Jesus.[5] I couldn't see it at the time, but looking back, I can see and that strengthens my faith every time. What a treasure!

Shame first started to define me at my conception. For much of my life, I had been convinced that my life was not intentional. My mom was nineteen when I was born. Her dad, my grandfather, was an old time Vermont meat cutter. My grandmother was a devoted wife and mother, raising six children in the Depression age. My father was a twenty-nine-year-old trumpet-playing bartender from Detroit, Michigan. It's hard for me to believe that the match between my mother and father was celebrated by my mom's family, but in those days, what choice did they have? My father struggled with substance abuse, and my mom made a career of maintaining our cover as the perfect family. Was I a mistake? Was I the cause of all the chaos and anger in my family? Not according to this truth.

"For You created my inmost being; You knit me together in my mother's womb. I praise You because I am fearfully and wonderfully made; Your works are wonderful; I know that full well."[6]

But here I was. My mom worked full time and my father was volatile and unpredictable. I found comfort and security in food. I was chubby when chubby was not acceptable. Yes, my clothes were even labelled "chubettes." I was ridiculed by my peers, always the last one chosen for any team, just never good enough. People would say, "You would be so pretty if you lost weight." My uncle told me he would buy me a hot fudge sundae if I lost weight. Shame, shame, shame.

The truth?

---

[4] Genesis 50:20
[5] Romans 8:29
[6] Psalm 139:13–14

"The Lord does not look at the things people look at. People look at the outward appearance, but the Lord looks at the heart."[7]

I graduated from high school with no dating experience but with a life-long desire to become a nurse. So I headed off to nursing school in Springfield, Massachusetts. I was the "Vermont Maid" with braids and not a lick of street sense, thinking I was ready to experience life. Parties at Springfield College, drinking, pot, breaking curfew, so many opportunities presented themselves for disaster and the real potential to destroy my nursing career before it even started. Shame on me.

But this truth kept me safe in His plan, even before I acknowledged it: "The LORD will keep you from all harm—He will watch over your life."[8]

That's not to say He was pleased with many of my choices, but He had a plan for me. Shortly thereafter, I met Ernie. He was different than the other "men" I had met. His father was also alcoholic and his mother an enabler. He had just ended a complicated relationship and was certainly not looking for any new entanglements. But the more time we spent together, the more we wanted to be together. Both of us had grown up in the church but neither one of us knew about a relationship with Jesus. We married two years later, both delighted to be entangled! Our wedding was not about saying "yes" to the dress or going on an exotic honeymoon. We were delighted to be joined together until death do us part—though neither one of us could fathom *that* reality. We had found the greatest treasure on earth! We were grateful for this truth: "Every good and perfect gift is from above, coming down from the Father."[9]

We had three daughters in six years: Kellie, Heather, and Megan. We were living the dream, at least our dream! I had it all, a loving and devoted husband, three perfect children, and a part-time nursing career. What could be missing? But there was a yearning for something more. Our children were the ones who drew us to church.

---

[7] 1 Samuel 16:7
[8] Psalm 121:7
[9] James 1:17

After all, every "good" parent should bring their children to church. For shame if you don't! But it was the Holy Spirit Who drew me into a real, living relationship with Jesus as a young wife and mother. I chose to believe that God wanted a relationship with me through His Son, Jesus even though I could not begin to understand it or explain it. This relationship started out as a real hunger for the Bible that is still insatiable to this day. It was the perfect tool for the search. This is His truth: "I have loved you with a love that lasts forever. And so, with unfailing love, I have drawn you to Myself."[10]

After spending eleven years in Massachusetts, we had the opportunity to move back to Vermont. Why would I want to go back? It didn't make much logical sense, but God was ordering our steps.[11] I was still young in my faith, and Ernie was patiently and genuinely trying to understand. We chose to test our faith regarding the decision to move. We prayed together and agreed that if our house sold, then that would be our "sign" that we should move. Our house sold within the week, so we quit our jobs, packed up the babies and headed north, guided by this truth: "Whether you turn to the right or to the left, your ears will hear a voice behind you, saying, 'This is the way; walk in it.'"[12]

Vermont was good for the children and for us. The city had become a somewhat scary place for raising children and this was a much safer place for our growing family. Little did we know how much our family would grow! Ernie worked wherever he could to support us, and I found a per diem job in the NICU. In those days, jobs in the NICU were rare. Those who went to work there stayed forever. Ernie eventually found a steady job working with a passionate Christian man who was unashamed to share his faith. As much as he tried, Ernie could not ignore the truth that he was hearing daily. This man's passion was contagious, and the fire spread to all of us. Our faith was growing, and our children were growing up in the faith as well. This is where I decided to "do something good" for

---

[10] Jeremiah 31:3 New Living Testament
[11] Psalm 37:23
[12] Isaiah 30:21

God and run for school board. Long story short, I lost. I had failed. Shame on me. I had lived most of my life in performance mode. I thought that if I could do good and be good, I could have some control of my world. But the truth is "'For my thoughts are not your thoughts, neither are your ways my ways,' declares the LORD. 'As the heavens are higher than the earth, so are my ways higher than your ways and my thoughts than your thoughts.'"[13]

As I have already written, two months later, our fourth daughter, Jenna, was born; and we weren't even expecting. At the same time, my father and my brother, also an alcoholic, found AA. Things started to look up. My father was not doing well living on his own, so we built an in-law apartment onto the family home. Forgiveness had started its healing work. He was able to start a relationship with his granddaughters as well. All was well for eight months until I found that he had died of a self-inflicted gunshot wound in his little apartment. What had I missed? Shame on me! How could he do this? We couldn't tell anyone what really happened, it was too shameful. The word *father* literally repulsed me for a very long time. I imprisoned myself in an impenetrable fortress of self-protection. No one would ever hurt me *and* my family like that again!

My striving and my performance had failed miserably. I could not find my way out. It was here that God began to break down the walls that I had thought were protecting me. Instead, they were keeping me isolated and separating me from the love of my Heavenly Father. In the midst of this chaos, God reminded me of His commandment: "Honor your father and your mother, that your days may be long in the land that the Lord your God is giving you."[14]

That did not settle well. I railed against that and wrestled with God. I say I wrestled with God, but in reality, I was wrestling with myself and my inner dialogue that continued to deceive me. "Seriously? You want me to honor someone who has made a career out of destroying me and my family? You cannot be serious!" But serious, He was. God told me that I was to honor my father by lead-

---

[13] Isaiah 55:8–9
[14] Exodus 20:12

ing worship at his burial. My father did not deserve worship, but my God certainly did. I submitted and God was faithful to begin the slow process of healing and strengthening my faith to see Who He really is and what He can really do!

Shortly thereafter, I returned to work, still harboring my secret and terrified that someone would ask about my father's death. I was wound tightly in self-protection and had little if any reserve to support the families that needed it even more than me. I was assigned to a baby whose mother was known to be "prickly and controlling." She was desperately trying to control the outcome of her child and often engaged staff in power struggles to prove her control. Normally, I would have been able to counter her attacks with calm and quiet. This day, I had no reserve. We began to get into a power struggle about something and I found myself starting to engage. I caught myself and apologized, saying simply that I was having a hard day. She answered, "Well, we all have our problems." This comment seemed to minimize and trivialize all I was enduring. This was not going to end well, so I left the room to gather my composure. As I left the room, I was desperately praying for God to help me. Then I literally heard the voice of God say, "Forgive her." That was not the help for which I was searching!

What in the world! I had been the one wounded and I had to extend forgiveness? Come on! But being in the desperate state of trying to keep myself from completely falling apart, I submitted... again. This mother and I eventually developed a bond that kept us connected even after her child died and into the healthy birth of more children. Now, there's the treasure!

It was at this time that I went on parenting leave when Caitlin was added to our family, as explained in the chapter "The Gym." God was setting me aside to reveal Himself to me in a whole new way. It wasn't until I learned these truths could I begin to heal:

> And do not call anyone on earth "father,"
> for you have one Father, and He is in heaven.[15]

---

[15] Matthew 23:9

Therefore confess your sins (speak openly)
to each other and pray for each other so that you
may be healed.[16]

I began to see that my perception of my Heavenly Father had been distorted by my experience with my earthly father. I needed to know the truth. I needed to know *His* truth. This healing has been an ongoing process of prayer, confession, being washed in His Word,[17] and being transformed by the renewing of my mind.[18] Slowly and steadily God continues, even now, to correct my thinking to be in alignment with His. I am still a recovering control freak, but I can see the error of my ways much quicker now. He does not make demands on me merely to exercise His sovereignty but for my benefit, so I can live at peace with Him in this less-than-peaceful world. As I continue to search for His treasures, He continues to unearth them in His Word.

Parenting Caitlin has been a renewing process as well. It has required that I lay aside my pride. It has required me to deny the possibility that I might have a leg-up on parenting with child number five. It has corrected any erroneous thoughts that I may know something about raising children! I have had to change my expectations of her and my expectations of many others whom I have had contact because of her. She showed me that my neatly packaged world needed to be unwrapped to allow God to free me from my prison of expectation. She continues to teach me daily about patience, compassion, mercy, and genuine love and acceptance. A painful treasure. The truth?

"But God hath chosen the foolish things of the world to confound the wise; and God chosen the weak things of the world to confound the things which are mighty."[19]

Eight years into this new parenting learning curve, Ernie was diagnosed with malignant melanoma. He pursued every treatment

---

[16] James 5:16
[17] Ephesians 5:26
[18] Romans 12:2
[19] 1 Corinthians 1:27

available here in Vermont; at Dartmouth in New Hampshire; at the National Institutes of Health in Bethesda, Maryland; and at Memorial Sloan Kettering in New York City. He may have been the typical man-cold sufferer, but when it came to cancer treatment, he earned the nickname Brickhouse. Ernie's truth through three years of treatment was this: "I have strength for all things in Christ Who empowers me [I am ready for anything and equal to anything through Him Who infuses inner strength into me; I am self-sufficient in Christ's sufficiency]."[20]

Ernie knew where he was going but his heart broke over the thought of leaving us all behind. He fought for three years, never losing his hope and faith in his Lord Jesus Christ. He died at fifty-four. These truths are sometimes still hard for me: "The LORD gave, and the LORD has taken away; blessed be the name of the LORD."

"Shall we accept good from God, and not trouble?"[21]

I was now a widow and a single parent—double shame, unprotected, alone, destined to drown in an ocean of despair. But God… He carried us through graduations knowing how proud Dad would have been. We had weddings without the father of the bride and births without the grandpa. Treasures shrouded in pain. The truth?

"Be strong and courageous. Do not be afraid or terrified…for the LORD your God goes with you; He will never leave you nor forsake you."[22]

Every day I learn more about my everlasting, never-failing, perfect Father, Protector, Provider, and Beloved. Even after nineteen years, I still miss Ernie to the very core of my being, but the presence of Jesus within me allows me to carry on and face each new challenge in His power, not my own. These are great and eternal treasures.

> But He said to me, My grace (My favor
> and loving-kindness and mercy) is enough for
> you [sufficient against any danger and enables
> you to bear the trouble (wo)manfully]; for My

---

[20] Philippians 4:13 AMPC
[21] Job 1:21; 2:10
[22] Deuteronomy 31:6

strength and power are made perfect (fulfilled and completed) and show themselves most effective in [your] weakness. Therefore, I will all the more gladly glory in my weaknesses and infirmities, that the strength and power of Christ (the Messiah) may rest (yes, may pitch a tent over and dwell) upon me![23]

My shame continues to be demolished as I saturate my thoughts in His Word. It continues to cleanse me of the deception that hindered me and lead me in the freedom of my faith. It is the treasure of truth. This body is becoming less and less a shame bearer and more and more an image-bearer of my God and my Lord. As I allow His Word to change me, mentally and physically, I am progressively able to become the woman He created me. And my greatest joy is that it's never too late to become a new creation in Christ, His treasure for His glory!

I still struggle with shame and regret at times. My greatest wish is that I could have been the work in progress I am now when I was Ernie's "bride." I would have loved to share the freedom I have found in Christ with him and allow him to see beyond the walls I had built up. Ernie deserved so much better, but he loved me anyway. I am thankful that we will be reunited in heaven, and we will enjoy each other's perfection as we worship our Jesus together. While tears were not something that have come easily for me around my walls, I know that when we are reunited tears of joy will flow freely and unhindered. The tears that Jesus will wipe away will be tears of joy and happiness for all He has done. The ultimate treasure!

The truth is that I was intentionally created by God. He selectively chose me for His team and for His purpose. I am created and chosen to give Him glory and to show His power, His ability and His willingness to claim me as His own. And even though my outward self is aging and perishing, I do not lose heart as my inward self is

---

[23] 1 Corinthians 12:9 AMPC

being renewed day by day.[24] This quote by D. L. Moody says it all: "The world has yet to see what God can do with a (wo)man fully consecrated to Him. By God's help, I aim to be that (wo)man."

Your story will not be my story but perhaps there will be areas where you can insert your shame in mine and apply the truth of God's Word for deliverance. Scripture tells us, "And they overcame him by the blood of the Lamb and by the word of their testimony, and they did not love their lives to the death."[25]

It is my hope that the testimony of Jesus over my life and the words of His truth will give you hope for your future. No matter your origin, your path, or your perceived destiny, He can arrest it at any point and take you to Himself and restore you to wholeness. I am, clearly, a trophy of His grace alone. There was nothing inherent in me that was worthy of praise until He touched it for His glory and made it a treasure for Him!

Lord, thank You for Your truth that shatters shame. Thank You that You can take all my scars and scrapes and mold them into a vessel for Your honor, cleansed and set aside to be useful for You, prepared for every good work to which You call me.[26] Lord, I choose to daily yield my life to You.

> Do not fear, for you will not be ashamed;
>> Neither be disgraced, for you will not be put
> to shame;
>> For you will forget the shame of your youth,
>> And will not remember the reproach of your
> widowhood anymore. (Isaiah 54:4)

---

[24] 2 Corinthians 4:16
[25] Revelation 12:11
[26] 2 Timothy 2:21

EPILOGUE

Many years ago, God defined my life mission for me. It is this:

To impart, ignite and inspire wholeness (*shalom*[1]) among the spiritually oppressed.

My hope is this:

To impart: that these words will give you an added deposit of faith in what He can and will do on your behalf.

To ignite: that the Holy Spirit will breathe life into the deposit of faith that He has given you at your creation and He will set it on fire so that you can burn for Him.

To inspire: that these words will fan into flame the gift of God[2] in you.

We are all subject to oppression from our flesh, the world and the enemy of our souls. Every day I need to start afresh with Him. I need to push back the oppression with His Words of truth.

This is my history, His-story, my story for His glory. He has and will use His work in my life to encourage and comfort others. If my story can encourage just one other struggling soul, my mission will have been accomplished!

I pray that you, the reader and my new friend in Christ, will find the hidden treasures in your story. No matter the pain, no matter the mistakes, no matter the disappointment and disillusionment, He will bring treasures from it. We don't know why; we don't know when and we don't know how, but we know He will. If you have called on Him, He will answer because His Name depends on it. He will never fail!

Thank you for taking this journey with me. God bless you on yours!

---

[1]   Strong's concordance 7965 SHALOM
[2]   2 Timothy 1:6

ABOUT THE AUTHOR

A native Vermonter, Cindy is the bride to a husband in heaven, mom to five daughters, mother-in-law to four sons, and Mimi to six grandsons and two granddaughters. After Jesus, her family is her most treasured gift. A semi-retired NICU/pediatric registered nurse, she has seen the fingerprints of God all over her life. A lover of the Word and His Word for over forty years, she continues to find treasures hidden in that Word that give hope, encourage, renew the mind, and change the way she walks. This is a continuation of the hidden treasures found in her first book, *A Walk Through The Shadow*. She is a perfected work in progress, a grateful trophy of His grace alone.

Printed in the USA
CPSIA information can be obtained
at www.ICGtesting.com
LVHW040032120924
790640LV00002B/387

9 798893 096187